"HOW TO BE THE SUPER R(
MOM, SCOUT LEADER, SUND
ETC., ETC., ETC.

A JUNK DRAWER IDEA BOOK FOR MOM

by
Diane Sand

Creative Illustrations by Linda Lock
Lettering by Kim Stewart Arant

Published 1997
by
DLS SERVICES
4157 Signal Ridge Drive
Lilburn, GA 30047

"HOW TO BE THE SUPER ROOM MOTHER, TEAM MOM, SCOUT LEADER, SUNDAY SCHOOL TEACHER, ETC. ETC. ETC." Copyright © 1997 by Diane Sand. Printed and bound in the United States of America. All rights reserved. No part of this book may be reproduced in any form or by any electronic or mechanical means including storage and retrieval systems without permission in writing from the publisher, except by a reviewer, who may quote brief passages in a review. First edition.

ISBN 0-9663584-1-4

Publication #6690

Printed in the United States of America by:

G & R Publishing Company
507 Industrial Street
Waverly, IA 50677
800-383-1679
gandr@gandrpublishing.com
http://www.cookbookprinting.com

FOREWORD

"HOW TO BE THE SUPER ROOM MOTHER, TEAM MOM, SCOUT LEADER, SUNDAY SCHOOL TEACHER, ETC. ETC. ETC." was written to save young mothers many hours of searching for ideas for their children's activities. It is intended to help busy mothers do a SUPER job without taking too much of their precious time searching.

The ideas and recipes in this book are not my personal creations. They are a collection of my favorites while raising my children – Stephanie, Brad, Jeff and Rachel – over the past 26 years.

These ideas are designed for "MOM" to enjoy surprising the children with clever activities and snacks. I have many fond memories of working on these projects with friends and thank them for all their help and support. I hope this book will help you create special memories for you and your family and inspire your own creativity and generosity. Don't forget to take pictures!

I would like to thank my family for helping me remember some of these ideas and all the good times. A special thank you to my husband, Larry, who has tolerated the mess I always seem to have on the dining room table.

Diane Sand

Acknowledgments

My special thanks to these people who helped develop this idea book over the years on the dining room table.

PAULA YOUNG . . . the "cheerleader" who kept me going on this project.
CORENE MESSER . . . my sister who has sent me ideas for years.
KATHRYN BRUNSSEN . . . my mother who inspired me to put forth extra effort to make activities special for children.
CAROL SCHMINKE . . . my sister who forces herself to do these projects so she will be a good grandmother.
LINDA DUFFY . . . my sister-in-law who provided her business "know-how".
SHARON SAND . . . my sister-in-law who asks me for ideas for her young children and convinced me there was a need for this book.
MICHELLE MANNICK . . . a friend willing to share her knowledge and expertise.

Additional thanks to the following people for their friendship and encouragement, sharing ideas and contributing their valuable talents to different aspects of this book:

Dottie Cummins	**Kathy Pessolano**
Connie Frost	**Claudia Quarles**
Kathy Gingerich	**Peg Ruge**
Donna Greenmun	**Janet Neely**
Wanda Hewitt	**LuAnn Sand**
Ronda Ihrig	**Norene Sand**
Helen Lentz	**Patty Slocumb**
Judy Lock	**Stonemont Women's Club**
Jamie Moore	**Deanna Sup**

JUNK DRAWER IDEAS

"RAISING CHILDREN IS NOT FOR THE FAINT OF HEART."

Roz Chast

Table of Contents

PARTY TIME

Party Pointers .... 1 - 2
Centerpieces .... 3 - 5
Party Decorations .... 6 - 8
Creative Socials .... 9 - 11
A Party For Every Month .... 12 - 13
Banquets .... 14 - 19
Sleepover Parties 20
Birthday Parties .... 21 - 23
Classroom Parties .... 24 - 28

GIFT IDEAS

Thank You With A Smile 29
Hostess Gifts .... 30 - 31
Gifts For Family Away From Home 32
Family Touches - Gifts of Love .... 33 - 34
Family Rituals - Gifts of Time .... 35 - 37
Coach and Team Mother Gifts .... 38 - 39
Gifts and More Gifts .... 40 - 45
Gift Wrapping Made Fun .... 46 - 47

FUN FOOD (M-O-M = Master of Meals)

Mom, I'm Starved .... 49 - 68
Turn Ordinary Food Into Something Special .... 69 - 72
Decorating Cakes, Cupcakes .... 73 - 76
Cupcakes For Every Month of the Year .... 77 - 80
Breakfast Fun .... 81 - 86
Holiday Foods .... 87 - 114

HOLIDAY CRAFTS

Valentine's Day .... 115 - 117
Easter .... 118 - 121
Mother's Day 122
Father's Day 122
Halloween .... 123 - 126
Thanksgiving .... 127 - 128
Christmas .... 129 - 136

KEEP 'EM BUSY (M-O-M = Master of Mayhem)

Raising Children is not for the Faint of Heart .... 137 - 150
Mom, I'm Bored .... 151 - 152
Field Trip Adventures .... 153 - 154
Mom, Let's Play .... 155 - 156
This 'N That 157

PARTY TIME

PARTY POINTERS

- Begin planning early
- Be specific
- Pamper your budget
- Use a checklist
- Play great music
- Keep it casual
- Pay attention to colors
- Be imaginative and creative
- Have your party invitation resemble the front page of a newspaper
- Select your menu carefully
- Choose foods and garnishes which complement each other
- Take an inventory of supplies
- Arrange for help if necessary
- Use what you have – spray paint old baskets, etc.
- Break the rules – burn candles during the day
- Avoid "the same old thing" parties
- Remember people on special diets – especially children in the classroom
- Create an original invitation that ties in to the theme of the party

- Set the mood with fragrances – coffee, baking bread
- On hot days and nights, pass out small folding fans to your guests
- Fasten down tablecloths with reusable putty

- For inexpensive tablecloths use twin-size flat sheets – for matching napkins, cut off the sheet and zigzag the edges of the napkins
- Serve silverware for a buffet meal in brightly colored food cans with labels left on – be sure to file away the rough edges
- Keep your house smelling fresh by mixing 2 1/2 ounces of cinnamon oil with 10 ounces of rubbing alcohol – pour into a spray bottle
- Keep a fire extinguisher nearby when grilling
- Wrap flatware in a napkin and secure with a ribbon – put in a festive container for guests to pick up
- Put candles in the freezer for a few hours before your party to make them burn slower and drip less
- Pass out individually wrapped insect repellant towelettes at outdoor parties to keep bugs away
- When it comes to making a "big bang", popping balloons is unparalleled – and how much more fun if streams of confetti come pouring out – stuff as many confetti pieces or circles punched out of colored construction paper into deflated balloons using a funnel – blow up the balloons and hang high until time to hand out pins and let the confetti fly
- Send party invitations in cut-up puzzle form so person has to put puzzle together to read

- Glue shiny stars or various shaped confetti onto clear plastic glasses
- Relax and enjoy the party – your party mood and spirit will catch on

CENTERPIECES

This **indoor hot dog and marshmallow roast** is a great conversation piece. Hollow out a 4-inch styrofoam ball so a votive candle holder will fit into the hole. Sit the styrofoam ball on a candle holder to keep it steady. Cover the styrofoam ball with miniature marshmallows and miniature cocktail hot dogs on toothpicks. Light the votive candle for "roasting".

Use round, flattish bread as the base for centerpieces.

Attach **"theme" paper plates** that you are using for your party onto balloon sticks and then secure with heavy wrapping tape. Put the plates attached to sticks into a centerpiece with balloons. Perhaps into a top hat.

Fill a glass bowl with assorted **macaroni shapes.**

Put a **flower arrangement** in a chafing dish and sit on a mirror.

Place a **hurricane lamp** on a footed plate for an unusual look. Add decorations for the occasion.

Carve a design into a **watermelon**.

Transform **kitchen gadgets** into lanterns by placing votive candles inside them. Add bows and evergreen sprays.

Have a **balloon centerpiece** at parties with each child's name written on a balloon. When the party is over, let the child take their balloon home.

Spray **metallic gold or silver paint** on fresh fruits or vegetables such as squash, eggplant, asparagus, eucalyptus sprigs.

Your **festive centerpiece** is easy by filling a flat basket with greenery and then arranging hollowed-out oranges filled with votive candles in the basket.

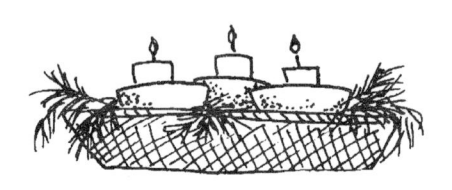

Select **small fruits** – tangerines, lemons, limes, small bunches of grapes. Dip each in egg white, then in granulated sugar. Set on waxed paper to dry. Place fruit in a glass bowl to display.

Make a **cranberry wreath centerpiece** by dipping cranberries in liquid floor wax. Use a food strainer to lower into wax and to drain afterwards. Secure cranberries to a foam wreath form with florist pins, toothpicks or straight pins to cover the surface. Attach sprigs of cedar and a bow. Place finished wreath on a cardboard circle to protect the table it is placed on. Add a hurricane chimney and candle in the center of the wreath.

You can vary your wreath decorations by using a **caramel popcorn mixture** and forming into a wreath shape. After dinner the guests can enjoy eating this centerpiece.

Make a **pasta bouquet**. Take thin and thick spaghetti and arrange it in a pitcher so that it fans out like a bouquet of flowers. Tie with a ribbon of red, white and green for an Italian touch.

Put a **cake on a footed cake stand** and it becomes an instant centerpiece. Add ivy and fresh strawberries around the stand.

For a **brunch centerpiece** put flowers in a porcelain teapot with some of the flowers flowing down into a tea cup and saucer.

Fill a **cornucopia** with pastries. Use toothpicks to make clusters of 3 to 5 donut holes.

For a **fresh fruit centerpiece**, pull a fresh flower through the center of a lemon or orange slice. Arrange decorated slices around the fresh fruit.

Divide a **pineapple** lengthwise, hull it and put it end to end with toothpicks. Let strawberries spill over, fanfold red and yellow apples that have been cored but not peeled and add grapes in clusters. Clean ivy until shiny and line the tray. Just before the guests arrive, mist the ivy and fresh fruits.

For a **Passover centerpiece** make an arrangement with the lamb bone, egg and root of horseradish on a wooden base.

Make an **igloo centerpiece** by combining flour, salt and water and mold over an inverted mixing bowl. Place in the middle of a piece of glass or mirror and outline edges with sugar cubes interspersed with floating candles. Use cotton batting to look like snow.

PARTY DECORATIONS

Make a **"PARTY" banner** that can be used for all types of parties.

Wrap plastic flatware for each individual with a **colorful pipe cleaner.**

Create **bread stick place cards**. Break bread sticks into varying sizes and hold together with a rubber band. Then tie a ribbon around for decoration. To stand up, insert broken toothpicks into the bottom of two of the bread sticks and attach to a slice of party bread. Decorate with a sprig of flowers and add a name card.

Fill a brandy snifter with **fortune cookies**. Set in the center of a table or coffee table. Tie with a bow and guests will love the conversation that follows opening the cookies.

Make a **display** with the party theme on a three-sided backboard.

When using a **paper tablecloth**, put plastic underneath to protect the table. Put the plastic over the tablecloth if you want to reuse the paper tablecloth.

Design your own **"money"** from photos, stickers, or drawings and run off copies to use for games or decorations.

A fun **place card** idea is an individual cookie for each child with his name written on the cookie in icing from a tube. You may let the children decorate their own cookies. Provide icing, a wooden stick, and decorations such as nuts, raisins, sprinkles, chocolate chips, coconut.

Put **styrofoam paper cups** in a preheated 200° oven for 10 seconds or until they melt down to resemble a hat. Remove from the oven and decorate for the appropriate occasion.

Decorate **clear plastic drinking cups** for each individual at the party with their name and party theme using paint pens.

Stencil **hurricane lamps** for interesting party effects.

Have all the **eating utensils** together before the party begins – paper plate, flatware, napkin. Cover with plastic wrap to keep clean. Tie with curly ribbon.

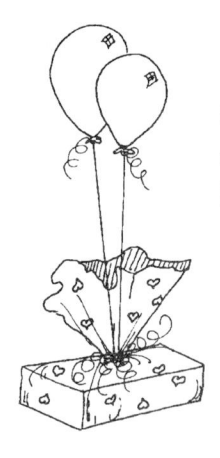

Use **balloon accents** around the party room. Wrap colorful cellophane around a brick. Tie with curly ribbon. Attach helium balloons.

Use **butcher paper** for the tablecloth and let the children draw on it. Have them draw their faces to mark their place at the table and write their name above the face.

Have children make **place markers** for the special meal. Cut a three-inch square out of posterboard or construction paper. Fold in half. Decorate with stickers of crayons. Write the child's name on the card.

For a buffet dinner party put **rolled napkins** in a basket that are tied and decorated with ribbons.

Make **party hats** using a cone shape. Decorate according to the theme of the party. Attach a cord or ribbon in 18-inch lengths to tie hats under their chins. Staple ribbon onto hat.

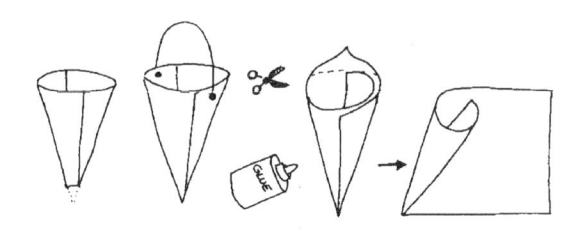

String **paper lanterns** in trees. Use strings of white Christmas lights around outdoor umbrellas and along fences.

CREATIVE SOCIALS

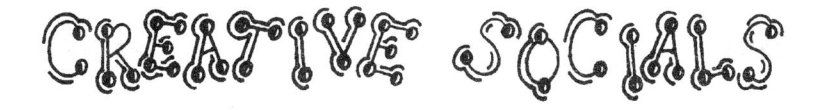

MAD HAT PARTY – Send an invitation in the shape of a hat. Have everyone wear a hat to the party. Give gifts for the prettiest, craziest, most original, etc. This is a good ice breaker at any type of party.

BACKWARDS PARTY – Send an invitation using a reverse carbon so the person receiving it has to hold it up to a mirror to read. Have the guests arrive at the back door and when they enter they must say "good-bye" and have them leave through the front door saying "hello". You can also have them walk into the house backwards. Have guests wear clothes backwards, spell names backward on name tags, serve food backwards – dessert first, etc. Play games backwards – pin the donkey on the tail.

TIE-DYE PARTY – Make tie-dye shirts. Use only 100 percent cotton items. They absorb the dye better than synthetics.

WESTERN PARTY – Send a covered wagon-shaped invitation. Wear coveralls. Cover your picnic table with brown paper. With black marker draw cowboy and Indian symbols (tepees, ten-gallon hats). Use red bandanas for napkins. Serve ranch burgers (roll ground beef into long portions to resemble a hot dog). Serve in frankfurter rolls. For dessert serve branded ice cream. Slice ice cream and with melted chocolate write initials to resemble brands. Have bales of hay to sit on. Use tin cans for vases; felt holsters to hold napkin and flatware. Pass out bubble gum cigars. Tie large pretzel sticks together for "logs" with ribbon for party favor.

GOURMET FOOD GIFT EXCHANGE – Have each guest bring food ready to eat during the party and one gift item that can be exchanged. Recipes should be included. (Bring your recipe in a clever card holder by wedging plastic foam into a clay pot, cover with artificial greenery and insert recipe into foam on a plastic card holder from florist.) Remember to have extra recipe cards on hand for any additional recipes the guests may want to copy. Number the gifts as the guests arrive and allow them to draw a number for the distribution of the gifts after everyone enjoys the gourmet tasting.

GO FISH – For a special bash – or splash – add goldfish to the guest list. On the table place small goldfish bowls filled with colored rocks and a goldfish. Just before the celebration carefully tuck the ends of ribbon from a few helium balloons into the rocks in the bowl or tape under the fishbowl itself. Let each child take home a goldfish as a party favor or if not enough for each guest, give as game prizes.

APRON PARADE – Have everyone wear an apron to a party where you have a cookie exchange, recipe exchange, etc.

OLD FASHION BOX SUPPER – Each female decorates the box she puts a supper in. Put no names on the boxes. Since the men select the boxes, decorate as attractively as possible. Use any box from a show box to diaper boxes. Place all suppers together. Each male takes a turn to select a box. The girl who packed the supper is his supper partner. Can make homemade ice cream afterwards.

Consider these: **EASTER "SUNDAE" OPEN HOUSE, JUNK FOOD POT LUCK GATHERING, PIG OUT PARTY, PINATA PARTY, EASTER EGGSTRAVAGANZA, BANANA SPLIT SOCIAL.**

A NIGHT FOR THE STARS

Draw a simplified solar system on a large sheet or piece of canvas using phosphorescent paint. Suspend it from tall poles over tables or cut shapes from posterboard and cover with aluminum foil so they "sparkle" and hang with fish line from ceiling.

Serve a **STAR SALAD:**

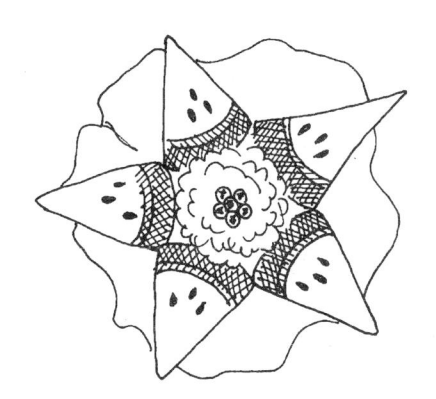

Cut five pieces of watermelon into triangles. Arrange on lettuce for individual serving in the shape of a star. Fill the center with cottage cheese and top with blueberries.

Have **STAR CANDY** sitting in baskets around the room.

STAR CUPCAKES:

Make a frosted cupcake. Cut out five red triangles from fruit leather and place in star shape on top of white frosted cupcake. Fill center area with blueberries.

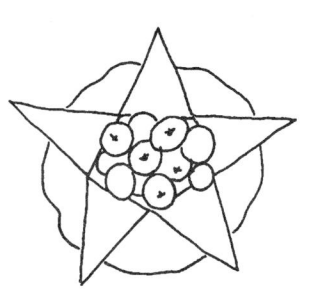

"There must be more to life than having everything."

Maurice Sendak

A PARTY FOR EVERY MONTH

JANUARY – **Superbowl!** Send out football-shaped invitations on brown paper with white markings. Dress in favorite sports clothes. Small foam footballs make inexpensive party favors. Use an old football helmet with balloons tied to it for a centerpiece. Prior to the big game show a sports blooper video.

FEBRUARY – Have a **King and Queen of Hearts party.** Guests should arrive in royal attire. Upon arrival present each guest with homemade paper crowns that you add glitter, buttons, faux jewels to. Use heart-shaped containers for party favors. Hire a caricature artist for the entertainment.

MARCH – March winds. This is the month for **flying kites**. Visit a local weatherman at a television station or have him visit your group. Perhaps make your own kites and then go fly them.

APRIL – "April showers bring May flowers." So now is the time to have a **garden party**. Have an exchange of seeds. Use clay pots as party favors. Perhaps decorate the pots with nontoxic paints for entertainment. Serve dessert in a large clay pot and scoop out with a small gardening spade.

MAY – Let's have a **picnic**. Think about all the traditional picnic necessities – checkered tablecloth, frisbees, blankets on the grass. Munch on "ants on a log" (celery, peanut butter, raisins), animal crackers, spider cookies (chow mein noodles, butterscotch and chocolate chips) and bug juice (green drink).

JUNE – We all scream for **ice cream**! Make homemade ice cream, have a sundae party with all the trimmings. June is National Dairy Month. Have old-fashioned floats in parfait glasses.

JULY – Hold your own **Fourth of July parade**. Have everyone make a festive costume, decorate wagons and bicycles. March around the neighborhood carrying a tape recorder of marching band music. Serve cookie pizzas with whipping cream, strawberries and blueberries on top.

AUGUST – **Beach party**. Send out fish-shaped invitations. Fill kiddie pool with sand for building and castles. Distribute leis to wear, decorate with palm trees. Turn on the sprinkler, toss beach balls, throw water balloons.

SEPTEMBER – Cool weather brings thoughts of fall leaves and **camping**. Set up tents in the back yard. Jump into piles of leaves. Build a campfire. Roast hot dogs and marshmallows. Tell ghost stories.

OCTOBER – Have a **masquerade party**. Carry out party with a mystery theme. Create a carnival-type atmosphere and serve witches brew.

NOVEMBER – Have a **holiday feast**. Invite a Native American to visit in tribal costume if you know someone or rent a video on Indian heritage and customs. Make necklaces of cranberries and popcorn.

DECEMBER – Hold a **tree-decorating party**. Have each guest bring a homemade ornament. Perhaps decorate ornaments at the party – two per person, one for the tree, one to take home.

SPORTS BANQUETS

Clever **placemats** for banquets can be cut from posterboard into the shape of appropriate sport. Add needed detail lines with round-tipped marker. During the season take snapshots of all the members of the team. Place several snapshots on each collage and then laminate. Be sure to put the team member's name, the year and team name. This makes a great conversation piece as well as keepsake.

Make party favors which can double for a Christmas **tree ornament** by using a round clothes pin. Paint in appropriate team colors. Put players name and number on "uniform". Drill a small hole for pipe cleaner arms.

For a **football centerpiece** use an old football helmet. Add a chrysanthemum, spirit flag and a few leaves.

Make **tree ornaments** for your sports team. Cut ball shape out of a thick wood. Paint to look like the ball would look. Add the child's name and/or number. Drill a hole for a string to hang.

For **sports banquet momentos** attach each child's picture to the front of a styrofoam ball. Put a hat and bandana on top of the ball for each individual table favor.

Make **sports picture frames** by cutting appropriate sports designs out of wood leaving a space for the child's photograph. Paint as desired. Can use same idea with poster board.

Have a **slide show** or video set to appropriate music at the end-of-the-year banquet with pictures taken during the season.

Put cupcake stick decorations into **sandwiches** served at banquets representing the sport honored.

For water related banquets perhaps have a decorating party for the entertainment of **personalizing life jackets**. Decorate as desired with fabric paint.

Make a **"golf dog paperweight"**. Hot glue seven old golf balls together into the shape of a dog. Add tee for the tail, felt for features and a small hat to complete.

A **wooden sports paperweight** is a great momento. Cut and stain a piece of wood the size of snapshots. take a photo of each player during season. Attach photo to wood and then heat seal with decoupage.

Make a **table centerpiece** a cut-out of a schoolhouse personalizing with the school name.

For a **track banquet** paint running shoes across the top of the paper tablecloth. Make batons out of PVC pipe and put child's name on individual baton.

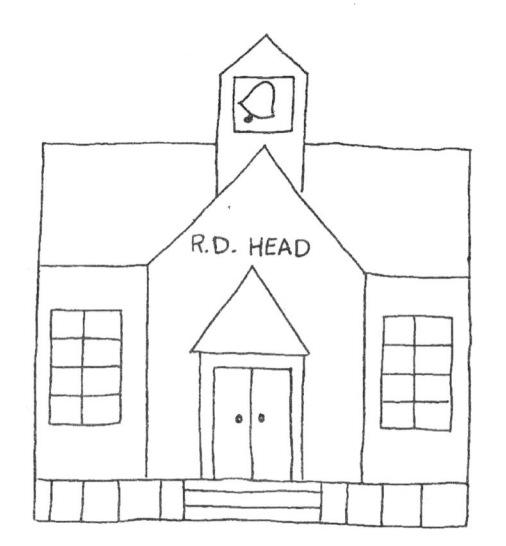

Play a **balloon game** at banquet. Divide group into equal teams and determine a goal line. The first person on each team gets on their hands and knees and blows the balloon to the goal line and back. This continues until one team finishes first.

Another **balloon game** is to divide guests into two teams and mark off opposite goals. Dump 20 balloons (10 each of a single color) in the center of the playing area. Use newspaper bats to sweep their team's colored balloons into their own goal.

Decorate the side of a **drinking cup** with a face by putting your finger in icing and attaching raisins, chocolate chips, etc. on the side of each child's cup.

Use a **fresh pineapple** and attach sports theme items with fresh fruit for table decoration and appetizer.

Use two clear **glass plates** to serve on. Put a sports decoration in between the glass plates such as paper soccer ball.

Honor graduates at banquets with a **graduation silhouette** in the shape of a boy or girl graduate. Cut an oval opening in the center of silhouette for child's picture.

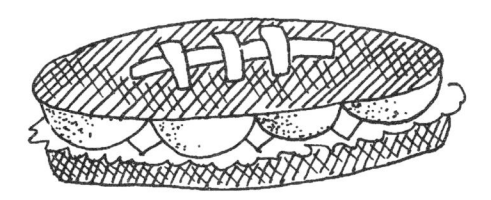

Serve a **football hero sandwich**. Use a large loaf of pumpernickel bread about 10 inches long. Cut the bread lengthwise. Arrange cheese and cold cuts on the bread. Prepare a dressing of 3 tablespoons of Russian dressing and 3 tablespoons of yellow mustard and spread on bread. Arrange strips of cheese on top of the bread in a lace-up fashion. Place under broiler for short time so cheese will adhere to bread.

Referee's Sandwich

4 1/2 ounce can deviled ham
1/2 teaspoon prepared mustard
1 1/2 teaspoon horseradish
1 Tablespoon chopped ripe olives
1 Tablespoon minced celery
Mayonnaise
5 slices dark bread
5 slices white bread

Mix all ingredients except mayonnaise and breads. Lightly spread the mayonnaise on all the bread slices. Divide the sandwich mixture evenly on the dark bread slices; then top with the white bread slices. Trim crusts, and slice in 3 or 4 long strips. Place the sandwich on a serving tray, alternating the light and dark bread to give the appearance of a referee's shirt.

QUARTERBACK SCRAMBLE

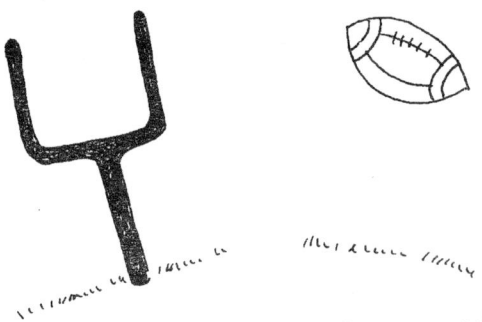

1/2 cup butter
1 package taco seasoning
4 cups corn cereal
4 cups wheat cereal
1 cup beer nuts
1/3 cup beef jerky, sliced
1/4 cup grated American cheese

Preheat the oven to 250 degrees. Melt butter in large shallow roasting pan in the oven. Remove. Stir in seasoning. Add cereal and nuts. Mix until all pieces are coated. Heat in the oven for 45 minutes. Stir every 15 minutes. Add beef jerky and cheese. Stir to coat evenly. Bake an additional 15 minutes. Spread on absorbent paper to cool. Makes 9 1/2 cups. **Put in packages with recipe for coach's gift**.

BASEBALL CAKE

Prepare a yellow cake mix as directed and bake in a greased and floured jelly roll pan for 20 to 22 minutes. Cool 10 minutes. Remove from pan and finish cooling.

Baseball Mitt – Place right hand on left side of cake and trace around it. Enlarge size of fingers and extend to make a mitt about 9 1/2 inches from fingers to wrist. Cut around outline. Hollow palm of mitt slightly. Cut licorice rope candy into short strips and lay between fingers for laces. Use a caramel icing.

Baseballs – From remaining cake, cut baseballs using 2 or 2 1/2-inch round cutter. Ice with white icing. Draw stitching lines on baseballs with caramel icing. Place ball in the palm of the mitt.

MUSIC BANQUETS

Hang **straw wreaths** from the ceiling light fixtures, etc. Attach miniature musical notes, band instruments and curly ribbon in color scheme.

Make a **musical runner** by using old sheet music. Curl on opposite ends and singe the edges for antiqued look. Decorate with tall candlesticks that have musical notes dancing up and down made from colored pipe cleaners.

Make a **cake** that is decorated with musical notes or instruments. Draw with icing a treble clef and staff (5 horizontal lines with 4 spaces in between). Press small gumdrops into oval shapes and place on lines to resemble notes of the song. Place birthday candles to the right of the gumdrop notes to complete the look of musical notes whether actually used for a birthday or not.

Play games that **identify songs** or have a dance contest.

If this is a party for a band group have each guest bring their **instrument** and each participate in playing something on their instrument.

SLEEPOVER PARTIES

Play a **toilet tissue get acquainted game**. Pass a roll of toilet tissue around the room and simply say "Take as much as you need". When everyone has torn the tissue off the roll, ask guest one-by-one to hold out two fingers and wrap the tissue around their fingers as they talk about themselves. They cannot stop talking about themselves until all their tissue is wrapped around their fingers.

Have all the guests write a message on the **pillowcase** at a sleepover. Remember to use a permanent marker.

Turn out all the lights and burn candles while telling **make-believe stories**.

Make **t-shirt sleepshirts**. Get large-sized t-shirts and add lace for trim. Paint with fabric paint or have party guests sign each shirt.

Go **caroling for shut-ins** and then have a make-your-own pizza party.

Go on an **audio scavenger hunt**. Instead of the traditional scavenger hunt, have one that you must get particular sounds on a tape recorder or video camera. Ideas for the hunt: dog barking, baby crying, sound at bowling alley, someone burping, woman screaming, policeman reading you your rights, siren, cat meowing, cheerleader doing a cheer, go to Chinese restaurant and have waiter say something in Chinese.

BIRTHDAY PARTIES

Balloons and parties go hand-in-hand. Balloons are inexpensive and instantly create a party atmosphere.

Use good **quality balloons** as the cheap ones lose air faster and are harder to inflate.

Be creative – send your party invitations in balloons, play games with balloons. Even if you are not real creative, a group of kids and a few dozen balloons scattered on the floor are a party all by themselves. Remember to keep balloons in your pocket while traveling. They may "save the day" with unruly children in the airport lobby when your flight has been delayed.

A great **birthday ice cream treat using balloons** can be made by poking a hole in the bottom of a paper cup and pulling about 12 to 15 inches of ribbon through. Leave the ribbon in place and fill the cup with ice cream. Freeze until ready to serve. At serving time, tie a helium balloon to the top of the string. Pull the bottom string until the balloon almost rests on top of the cup. Let the children cut their balloons free or pop them to get to the ice cream.

Create **crazy balloons** by placing a handful of beans in a balloon before you blow it up. Have the children stand in a large circle and bat the balloon to each other. If the balloon reaches the ground, the last child who touched it is out. The last child in the circle is the winner.

Bake a cupcake in a birthday ceramic coffee mug. Add a candle. **Cake and gift all in one**.

Put **sparklers** on birthday cakes.

Have a **mini-meal** birthday party for small children – mini pizzas, mini hot dogs, mini cupcakes, etc.

The number of children invited to your child's **birthday party should correspond with the age of the child** as a rule of thumb – 2 friends for a 2-year-old, 3 friends for a 3-year-old and so on until the child is older and accustomed to larger organized groups.

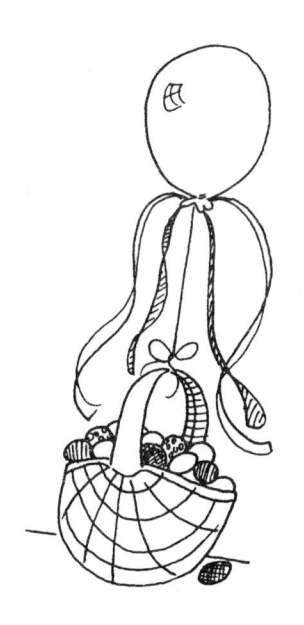

Serve a childhood favorite – **fluffernutter sandwiches** (peanut butter and marshmallow cream on bread).

Use brightly colored **cookie cutters** as napkin rings for your birthday party table setting. Let the guests keep the cutters as momentos of your party.

Put party information on pieces of paper, put the paper into balloons, blow up and deliver for your **party invitation**.

Kids love **shaker pompons** out of newspapers – roll newspaper, cut into strips – all except the end which will be taped and used for the handle.

Choose a birthday party theme and stick with it:

Baseball – Make a cake or cupcakes with child's favorite team emblem. Decorate with those colors. Use emblem or paper baseballs to decorate. Use baseball cards as favors. Make up games with a baseball theme or play baseball.

Sixteen-Year-Old – Make a cake or have one made to look like a driver's license. Have decorations made out of posterboard to resemble road signs. Play a game to see how many can recognize sign shapes.

Circus – Make a cake with any part of the circus theme. Put animals crackers on top of the cake. Have a friend dress up as a clown and come to the party to give away balloons, or perhaps, make animals shapes out of balloons. Serve cotton candy. Paint children's faces.

Doll – Have a cake in the shape of a favorite kind of doll. Have each child bring along their favorite doll. Set up a child's table to seat the dolls if you don't have a lot of guests. For party favors, buy inexpensive matching bracelets for the child and for their doll or perhaps make some type of bracelet as an activity. Decorate with any dolls and their accessories.

Up, Up and Away – Create a theme on flight. Use airplane favors. Perhaps visit the local airport. Make a hot air balloon cake. Prepare cake as directed. Bake in two 9-inch pans that are round and one 8 x 4-inch loaf pan. When baked, ice cakes as a hot air balloon would look. Attach balloon cake to basket cake using string licorice.

CLASSROOM PARTIES

FEED THE BIRDS . . . . Have children string popcorn, cranberries to hang on a tree for the birds to eat. Make peanut butter pine cones (spread peanut butter on pine cones and roll in bird seed). Take all outside and hang on a tree for the birds and children can watch.

SNOWBALL TOSS . . . . Glue cotton balls onto 3-inch styrofoam ball to look like a large snowball. Hang wreath in a doorway. Use masking tape to mark a line on the floor to stand behind. Try to throw "snowball" through the wreath while standing behind the line.

CLASSROOM PATCHWORK CAKE . . . . Have each child bring in the same size square or rectangular cake decorated as they would like or for a special theme. Assemble into a classroom patchwork cake. Invite other classrooms to help eat the cake quilt.

PRETZEL ABC . . . . Play ABC games with large pretzel sticks. The sticks make large letters and can be eaten as a reward.

DECORATE COOKIES . . . . Easy with refrigerated dough straight from the supermarket.

FEED THE ELEPHANT . . . . Draw a colorful elephant and hang on the wall. Put a basket underneath the elephant. Let the child give the elephant a peanut in a shell every time the child answers correctly. All can enjoy the peanuts when finished.

BOWL 'EM OVER . . . . Place 10 plastic soda bottles in line for bowling pins. Bowl with a soft ball.

HIDDEN NOISE GAME . . . . Have children sit where they cannot see you. Have them identify the noises they hear – pouring water, egg beater, snapping fingers, crumpling paper.

SNOWBALL FIGHT . . . . Give each child two large puffs of cotton batting and let them throw them at each other.

DRAW MYSELF . . . Have children draw themselves. Roll out freezer paper on the floor the length of each child. Have an adult trace child as they lay on the paper. Then have child decorate "person" to look like themselves.

NOODLES OF FUN . . . A package of alphabet noodles can give children many hours of fun and help with learning words. Glue letters to popsicle sticks for name pins.

PEANUT HUNT . . . . Hide peanuts in shells and have a hunt.

BALLOON BLANKET . . . Blow up three or four helium balloons for each child and contain them underneath a large sheet or bedspread. Have the children stand on the corners of the sheet to help hold it down. One by one, the children wiggle under the sheet and see how many balloons they can crawl out with without letting go. The winner ends up with the most balloons.

CANDY BINGO . . . . Give each child the same number of pieces of candy. Play bingo using candy as play pieces. When the game is over, child can keep candy.

COTTON BALL GAME . . . You will need: 1 shallow bowl, cotton balls, spoon, blindfold, stop watch and small rug if no carpeting. The bowl is placed on the rug and cotton balls are scattered around the bowl. Each person in turn is blindfolded, given the spoon and placed on the floor in front of the bowl. The person, using only the spoon, must get as many cotton balls into the bowl as possible within the time allotted, 1 to 2 minutes.

SILHOUETTES . . . . Spend an afternoon making silhouettes of each other. Position person between a light and a wall so the profile shadow is projected onto the wall and trace around the profile outline with a pencil. Cut out the silhouette, trace around it on black paper and cut out. Mount the black head onto white paper.

ANIMAL PARADE . . . . March around as a bunny, an elephant, a dog, a snake, a kangaroo, a bird, an alligator, etc.

BALL ROLL . . . . With children sitting in a circle and legs apart, roll a ball from one child to the next.

STORY TELLING . . . Using book as a reference or from your imagination, tell stories. Try to keep each child's story short.

KANGAROO RACE . . . Hop, holding a balloon between your knees, from one side of the room to the other.

MUSICAL CHAIRS . . . . The traditional way or passing a special item, the holder of item when the music stops is "out".

DRESS UP . . . . Offer a variety of clothes, hats, shoes, etc. that they all race to get into as quickly as possible. Makes great pictures.

SONGS . . . . Hokey-Pokey; London Bridge; Farmer-in-the-Dell; Eensy-Beensy Spider; Ring-Around-the-Rosy.

PIN THE TAIL ON THE DONKEY . . . . Or the nose on the bunny or beard on Santa – coordinate with occasion.

WALKING STICK . . . . Take a walk in the woods and find a sound tree limb one-inch or more in diameter. Interesting "handle" bends near one end are more fun. Use a rasp to remove the back and then sand the staff smooth, following the grain of wood. Cut to a convenient height. You can carve a design on cane, if desired. Rub on a coat of penetrating oil. Makes a great gift for children to give.

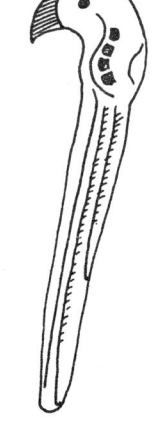

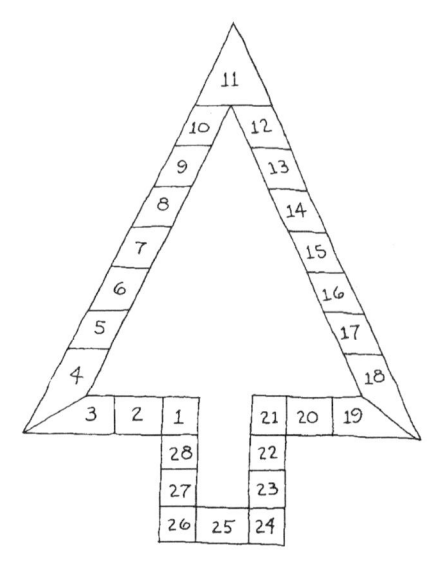

MUSICAL CHRISTMAS TREE WALK

Use masking tape to mark off large spaces in the shape of a tree on the floor. Tape sheets of construction paper that have been numbered consecutively onto spaces. Start the music. As music plays, the children march around the Christmas tree as in a cake walk. When the music stops, a number is drawn from the box. The child on the number called gets the prize.

DO ANIMALS FLY GAME
Best for ages 5-6.

Have the children stand or sit in a semi-circle facing you. Explain that you will call out something like "robins fly" and that every child must flap his arms like wings. However, if you say "elephants fly" then no one should wave his arms. Practice a few times using names of animals that do or do not fly so children understand what to do. When you start any child who does not wave his arms when you mention an animal that can fly is out. Any child who waves his arms when you call out an animal that cannot fly is also out. Call out animals names as rapidly as possible for children. Play until only one child is left.

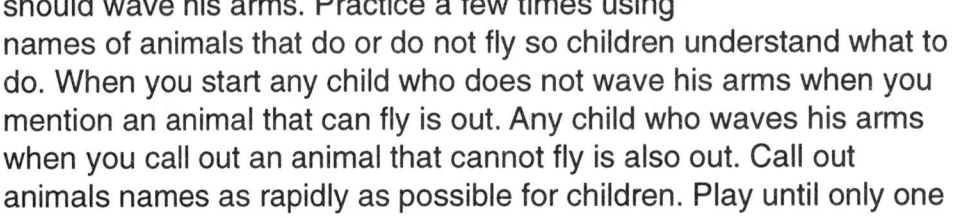

DOGGIE, DOGGIE WHO'S GOT THE BONE? . . . .
Children sit in a circle, one in the center is blindfolded and an object is given to one child, then all children put their hands behind their back and the group recites, "doggie, doggie . . . ." With the blindfold off, the child now is given 3 chances to guess who has the bone.

GIFT IDEAS

THANK YOU WITH A SMILE

1. Package of Light Bulbs – **"Thanks for lighting up our lives."**

2. Jar of Fruit Preserves – **"Thanks for getting us out of a jam"**.

3. Angel Food Cake – **"Thanks for being such an angel"**.

4. A Cassette Disc and Candy Bar – **"May your life be filled with music and calories"**.

5. A Handwritten Letter – A handwritten letter reaches out in a personal way and can be reread and treasured for years.

6. Homemade Soup – **"Thanks for being a 'souper' friend"**.

7. Jar of Mixed Nuts – **"I'd go nuts without you"**.

8. Peach Preserves – **"You are a peach"**.

9. Sewing Kit – **"SEW glad we are friends"**.

10. Homemade Cake – **"You take the cake"**.

11. Write your party thank yous on the back of a paper napkin from the restaurant where the party was held.

12. Use a blank notecard. Stencil to decorate around the following poem:

    **NOT WHAT WE GIVE,
    BUT WHAT WE SHARE
    FOR THE GIFT WITHOUT
    THE GIVER IS BARE.**

    Add your personal message on the back of notecard.

HOSTESS GIFTS

Frame an old **doily**.

Homemade **spices** in a crock.

Games for the family to enjoy.

Flower bulbs in a planter.

Homemade jams and jellies or relishes in decorated jars.

Home grown **flower seeds** in a wine goblet.

Plant a **cactus garden** in a tea cup.

Homemade **fudge** on an antique plate with recipe attached.

Fill scallop shells that are sold in specialty shops with **chocolates**. Can set the candy in Easter grass in the shells.

Give **mustard** topped with miniature cheeses and crackers to jazz it up.

Wrap **popcorn balls** in colored plastic wrap. Tie with ribbons and bells.

Fill a stemmed wine glass or a small wine carafe with **homemade jelly**.

Fill a clear **lucite recipe box** with some goodies. Decorate box with paint pens.

Fill **apothecary jars** with colorful candy.

Guest soaps in an old saucer.

Tie a **bandana** around a loaf of bread.

Cookie cutters tied with ribbon appropriate to the season.

Mixed nuts in a gelatin mold.

Homemade **beverage mixes** in unusual jars or crocks.

Give a collection of your **favorite recipes** in an attractive binder or cover your own notebook with fabric.

Give **pressed flowers** by themselves or laminate onto posterboard – makes great book marks.

Tie a bow around the handle of a **large scoop** that is filled with goodies.

Fill a sea shell with a **seafood dip**. Cover with plastic wrap and a bow.

Line a basket with a colorful cloth. Fill with a variety of **muffins**.

Give a gift of a round **loaf of bread** tied up with a big bow and fresh flowers through the bow's center.

Fill a coffee mug with **special blend of coffee**.

Attach a **sprig of fresh tarragon** or basil to a fancy bottle of wine vinegar.

Flowers from your garden.

Attach **smoked sausage**, cheese and crackers to a cutting board.

At Christmas, fill a **stocking** with goodies.

Give a Christmas **ornament**.

GIFTS FOR FAMILY AWAY FROM HOME

Everyone loves to receive a surprise package. Send **"care" packages** to a grandmother in a nursing home, college student, your child in the military, a recent widowed aunt or anyone who may need a special uplift.

You do not have to spend a lot of money. Send **reminders of home** – autumn leaves from your yard dipped in paraffin keep their color and do not dry out; tape a recorded message from everyone in your family; newspaper articles.

How about a **Round Robin Letter Gift**? What could be less expensive and more appreciated than a round-robin letter from family and friends. Had a new baby: give surefire ways to quiet a crying baby. Get well wishes – tell of your own hospital experiences. Anniversary greetings – give tried and true solutions to having another anniversary next year. You get the idea – be creative!

No one appreciates a gift more than **"the gift of time"**. When you want something extra for a family member who is sick or elderly, consider one of the following:

       Over bed pockets to hold pencils, books, etc.
       Food for their special diet
       Manicure
       Perform household chores
       Reading aloud sessions
       Trip to the shopping center
       Send a monthly surprise package
       Video or movie
       Hair styling
       Massages
       Simple exercise routine together
       New colorful bedsheets
       Rich scented lotions

FAMILY TOUCHES – GIFTS OF LOVE

"One of the deep secrets of life," Lewis Carroll reminds us, **"is that all that is really worth doing is what we do for others."**

Send weekly **family newsletters**. Include something interesting about each member of the family and add some fun stuff, too. Keep the newsletters in a three-ring binder so visitors are welcome to read and write a note on blank sheets in the back. Elderly relatives who are house bound would especially appreciate this activity.

Have a **family tablecloth** to use during holiday and special gatherings. Whenever you use the tablecloth have each guest sign and date it. You can embroider over the signatures, if desired. The tablecloth will hold many happy memories.

Draw a **family tree** on the wall of a spare room. Attach old and new pictures on each branch of the tree to mark the passage of time and to highlight special occasions. This is especially good for a family who lives away from the core of the family to familiarize young children with their relatives.

A **family cookbook** is a delicious way to save and preserve family history over and over. Make photo copies of the friends and relatives you received special recipes from and place on your recipe card. You will remember that person in a special way each time you use their recipe.

Send your mother-in-law a **card** expressing your appreciation for raising such a terrific guy.

If a family member collects pens, baseball cards, etc. keep your eyes open at garage sales, flea markets, etc. and send them a **surprise**.

Have a **family "reunion"** with no traveling involved by sending a round-robin letter. One person starts it off by writing a few paragraphs of news, perhaps accompanied by a photograph, then sends it on. Have a list of who it should be passed on to so it makes a full circle.

At a family reunion allow some time for **"20 Questions"**. To get everyone started, pass around lists of questions such as "What are the two words that remind you of Grandad?" "Who inherited Grandma's cookie jar?"

Send grandparents or other relatives home-baked cookies with a surprise touch – your toddler's handprint baked into each. Little ones enjoy lending a **"helping hand"**.

As a **christening gown** is passed along to new infants, embroider each child's name and baptism date on it.

When your baby outgrows the special outfits received as gifts, **showcase these treasures** by dressing teddy bears or dolls and sit them around the nursery.

Whenever one needs to feel close to someone, all one has to do is **write a letter**.

Write a letter to your child on a regular basis or on special days of their life beginning at birth. The letters will reflect your child developing into a person and all the special people and events that affected their life. This will be a treasured diary when old enough to enjoy over and over. If you are not a letter writer, make a cassette tape.

Make a **holiday greeting card** with a personal message from each member of the family.

Write a **note from the "tooth fairy"** when you leave the monetary reward.

FAMILY RITUALS – GIFTS OF TIME

"Shared experiences bind us together and define who we are as a family," says Nancy Rubin. She further states that "rituals add depth and meaning to family life and are stamped in our memories long after we have passed through childhood".

Try some of these and develop your own – use your imagination. **Create rituals** to pass down through the generations just like you do with an old family recipe.

- Serve **green pancakes** on St. Patrick's Day.
- Have **hot chocolate and cookies** after the first snowball fight of the winter.
- Make homemade **Easter baskets**.
- A **homemade gift** from Dad or Mom is more of a treat for your child than any designer product.
- Let your child choose his **favorite cereal** for his birthday breakfast.
- Create a **special pillowcase** your child can sleep on every night.
- Take spring **nature walks**.
- Have a Labor Day backyard **barbeque**.
- Go for **brunch** at a restaurant on Saturday mornings.
- Have **bedtime rituals** " prayers, songs, stories.
- Take an **autumn ride** into the country to pick apples.

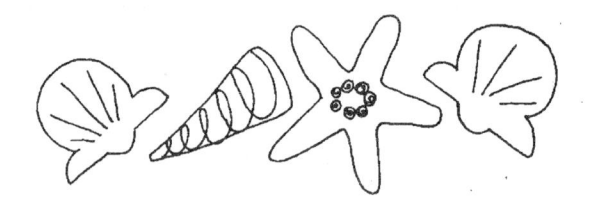

- Go for an annual visit to the **beach**. Save shells.
- Make the same **special recipe** on holidays.
- For a special start to a special day, **tie balloons to the bed** of the special person.
- Bake your own **festive bread** for Passover.
- Have Friday night be **"movie night at home"**. Turn off all the lights, serve popcorn in paper cups.
- Leave **messages** for the children on the bathroom mirror with shaving cream – parents never do that!
- Make a **time capsule** for your child (pay stubs, utility bills, dreams you have for the child, the parents courtship etc.)
- Keep a family **diary**.
- Save **t-shirts** from the child's activities and when graduates from high school make the shirts into a quilt
- Save a **calendar** from each year with activities of the family left on the calendar.
- Purchase a Christmas **ornament** each year for the child to take when has a home of his own.
- Keep the front page of the **newspaper** from each of your child's birthdays.
- Save favorite articles of clothing over the years and make into a **quilt**.
- Keep a school memories **scrapbook**.

- Write a **book** for your child – describe yourself as a child.

- Cook each child's **special meal** on their birthday or on special occasions. Serve on a special plate.

- **Make a tape** of you singing, telling a story or just talking to them so your child can listen to the tape in your absence.

- Send a **postcard** or letter to each child individually if you are on vacation, on a business trip or if the child is away at camp.

- Make **reprints** of favorite photographs as you take them and keep in a separate photo album for each child for when they leave home. Don't forget to date each photograph and write who is in the photo, location, etc.

- If you send **personal holiday greetings**, be sure to save one from each year as a keepsake for each child's scrapbook.

- When your child is learning their ABC's make an **alphabet game** with postcards from family members for your child. Send a message to friends and family assigning each a letter of the alphabet and ask everyone to send a postcard picturing something with their assigned letter. When you receive, punch holes in the upper left-hand corner and thread onto a key ring. You will have corresponded with family, gathered a great learning tool for your child as well as a special keepsake.

- Draw pictures or send **messages on a napkin** to put in your child's school lunch bag. Stickers make a great surprise message.

**"Life isn't a matter of milestones
but of moments."**

Rose Fitzgerald Kennedy

COACH AND TEAM MOTHER GIFTS

AUTOGRAPHED PHOTO

Take a photograph of the team. Purchase a light-colored mat and have all the team members sign the mat with their name and message.

MOM OF THE '90S

What could be more appropriate for a team mom than a wooden plaque, painting or needlework of "Mom" with a van loaded with children.

INDEX CARD BOOK

Purchase a photo album-frame combination. Put a picture of the coach or team mom in the frame. Have each team member and/or parents write a comment on a 3 x 5" index card. Insert these messages into the photo slots. Photographs from the season can be used to complete the album.

The same idea can be used but put the index cards into a decorated recipe box.

VIDEO POPCORN

Give unpopped corn as a gift in a clear video storage box. Decorate the video box with paint pens with team names, year, etc. or make a special label.

HER VERY OWN BUSINESS CARD

> 770-111-2222   "Tennis Nut"
>
> # LIZ ORRIS
>
> Wife and Mother Extraordinnaire
>
> Dependents: 333 Love Lane
> Jim, Ken, Barbara   Anywhere, TX

Have business cards printed for the "MOM" who devotes her time to youth and family. Add a comment in the quotation marks as to her particular interest. Dependents are the husband and children or could be team members. She will love giving to her friends, putting in her Christmas cards or using in volunteer activities.

HANDPRINT SHIRT

Using a plain colored t-shirt, have each child put their handprint on the front and back of shirt. Add name, age, year, team name. Put fabric paint on a paper plate for children to dip hands in.

BIG COOKIE GIFT

Bake your favorite drop cookie dough into plate-sized cookies and spread it out to one-half inch thickness. After baking and cooled, wrap and tie the big cookies with a ribbon. Can decorate cookies, if desired.

GIFTS AND MORE GIFTS

Fill a jar with round toasted oat cereal and attach a label that reads **"Bagel Seeds"**.

Give a gift of "money". This money actually being gold wrapped candy. Put the "money" in a burlap bag that has the words **"You Are Good As Gold"** stenciled on the bag or attach a card with the same message.

Encourage children to give **gift coupons** as gifts. Have them write out in their own handwriting. Examples would be: wash the dishes, prepare a bubble bath, free spring cleaning of a certain room, mowing grass, take a pet for a walk.

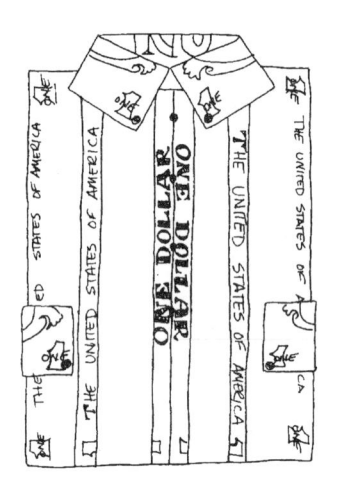

A **money shirt** can be given for all occasions and different size bills can be used on the back side. Cut a piece of posterboard 4 inches by 5 1/2 inches. Iron the edges of one-dollar bills to the back so the word "ONE" is on front. Fold each bill in half for the cuffs. Attach with removable tape. Cover the front and back of the posterboard with the ironed bills. Fold another bill in half and shape for the collar. Fold the remaining two bills into fourths for the front shirt ruffle. Attach buttons if desired.

Attach a special loaf of **bread** to a cutting board.

Give homemade frozen **cookie dough** wrapped and labeled with a cookie sheet and the recipe.

Decorate **acrylic picture frames**. Glue ribbon around the edges of the frame. Add a bow to upper left-hand corner and hot glue miniatures onto the ribbon. Use ribbon and miniatures coordinated with function.

Purchase plastic long-stemmed rose case from the florist. Place tissue paper in the bottom of the case. Fill with **sandwich cream-filled cookies**. Use paint pens to decorate for the occasion such as "Happy Birthday", "Get Well". Tie with curly ribbon to secure.

Make **name tags** out of various shapes in colorful paper, such as a shirt for Father's Day. Simply punch a hole in the corner and tie to package. Don't forget pinking shears for different effect when cutting.

Give packages of flower or vegetable seeds as a **springtime gift**. Flower bulbs are great for the fall.

Share your **garden produce** by adding fresh garden vegetables to a new shiny colored colander for a gift.

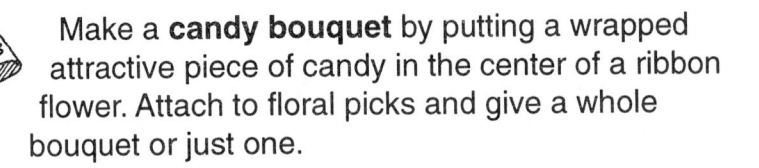

Make a **candy bouquet** by putting a wrapped attractive piece of candy in the center of a ribbon flower. Attach to floral picks and give a whole bouquet or just one.

Cut out various shapes from old **countertop** and use as a cutting board.

Purchase a plain **barbeque apron**. Then stencil the words "Main Squeeze" on the front. Fill pockets with barbeque sauce, utensils, etc.

What's Your Name? Make an album for someone that contains a collection of information on the history of their name. Do biographical information on people famous and not-so-famous that have the same name. Take photographs of friends who share their name. Give family history of any relatives who may share the first name.

Need a **moving gift**? Take a photograph of the moving person's home and have it enlarged. Purchase a light-colored mat. Have all the neighbors sign the mat and give as a going away gift.

New neighbor moving in? Don't forget to take the time to be neighborly. Stop by with a plate of goodies with a note attached:

> **Dear Friend:**
> **I know you're unpacking**
> **With chores galore,**
> **If you need any help,**
> **I live next door.**

Send fabric squares to baby shower guests and ask them to decorate the square with embroidery or fabric paint. Assemble into a **baby quilt**.

PERSONALIZE, PERSONALIZE

Personalizing makes the ordinary special. The designs can be very simple and paint pens are inexpensive. Perhaps iron on letters.

TOTE BAGS   TACKLE BOX   APRONS

BABY BONNET   NAP MATS

CUP   BOOKENDS   MUGS

PICTURE FRAMES   VISORS   PILLOWS

DIAPER SET   PURSES

TOOTHBRUSH HOLDER   T-SHIRTS

WASTEBASKET   TOWELS & WASHCLOTHS   STOOL

SWITCHPLATES   SWEATSHIRTS

TINS   BACKPACK

HAND HELD MIRRORS   FLOWER POTS

NAME PLAQUES   BIBS

OVERNIGHT KITS

HAIR RIBBONS   GARDEN GLOVES

TOOL BOX   CASSETTE CASES   SEWING KIT

PANTIES   CRAYON HOLDERS

Put real **tree branches** into a bucket filled with sand. Spray paint the branches, if desired. Decorate the branches with bows, curly ribbon, small gifts. Can be designed for any occasion.

Don't forget to give **live trees** as gifts. The special occasion will continually be remembered as the tree grows.

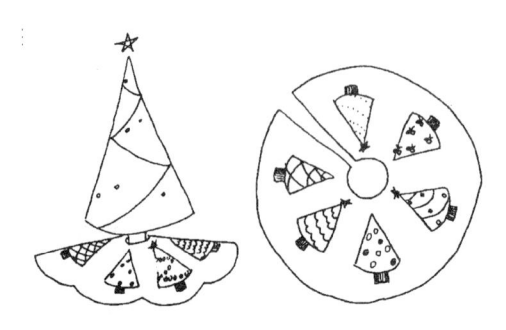

Work with the art teacher at school and have them each decorate a felt tree with sequins, paint, buttons. Sew a simple tree skirt and then using adhesive fabric attach each child's tree to the **tree skirt**. Can be used in the classroom during December and then given to the teacher as a gift.

Bookstores sell books listing the addresses of **famous people**. Send a request to favorites asking them to remember a friend or relative on a special occasion. Many, but not all, will respond.

Decorate a shirt with a saying that is appropriate for that person.

Have an artist draw **sketches** of someone's childhood home, church, school, office.

Hot glue **seashells** from a beach visit into a miniatures case.

Give a **holiday food wreath**. Attach an assortment of foods such as colored pasta, cookies, foil-wrapped candies, tiny jars of jam, gingerbread men, candy canes onto wreath. Add a bow or ribbons in the empty spaces of the wreath.

Give a **gift of candy**. Use individually wrapped candy only. Purchase a soda fountain glass. Fill the glass with some candy. Cut a styrofoam ball in half a and insert into glass. Then attach each piece of candy with a straight pin. Insert bows in between candy pieces.

Let your child design a quilt or **wall hanging** using fabric crayons (available at fabric shops) onto plain fabric. Have each grandchild design a square. Perfect for grandparents.

Make up a fun **basket of goodies**. Attach a note to each item. Jar of pickled bologna – "**You are full of baloney**". Bottle of glue – "**When you feel like you are falling apart, take two tablespoons and go to bed**". Container of thumb tacks – "**In order to keep you on your toes, step on these once daily**". Can of oil – "**When your knees and elbows feel achy**". Chocolate pudding, chocolate cookies, chocolate pie mix, fudge topping – "**Don't neglect the four basic food groups**". A book on aging and a package of prunes – "**Here is great advice to keep your mind full and your bowels empty**". Bottle of gin with the word "ESTROgin" written on it – "**This will replace your liver spots with youthful freckles**". Lucite container filled with gold wrapped chocolate coins – "**You are worth a million**". Glass container filled with candy – "**Wishing you sweet success**".

For a **wedding shower** start the bride and groom's first photo album with childhood photos of both that you gathered. Include an address book that has been filled with addresses and phone numbers of family and friends.

GIFT WRAPPING MADE FUN

Cookie Cutter Gift Wrap – Design gift wrap using brown paper bags and cookie cutters. Dip cookie cutters into tempera paints and stamp onto brown bag.

Paper Doll Effect Gift Wrap – Use old wrapping paper to cut out paper dolls, Christmas trees or any other shapes. Be sure to leave sides attached for the paper doll effect. Glue onto brown paper bag for a three-dimensional look.

Happy Hands Gift Wrap – Have children dip hands into tempera paint to design wrapping paper or gift bags.

Disguise your gift:

- add cardboard wings, legs, etc. to the outside of package.

- hide gift in yards of ribbon or popcorn

- hide gift in the house and then compose clues to find the gift. Wrap up the clues instead of the gift.

Vary from the traditional wrapping paper with:

- colorful Sunday comics
- felt designs
- leftover wallpaper
- old maps
- old Christmas cards cut up and add to packages for a decorative touch
- spray painted designs on brown packaging paper
- stencil designs on plain paper
- add flowers, leaves, cut-out figures, feathers to packages
- write greeting with glue on paper and then sprinkle glitter onto glue
- trim package with a small gift or ornament
- wrap gift in inexpensive fabric rather than paper

Instead of the same old box, try:

- paper towel roll
- panty hose "egg"
- large plastic soda bottle – cut in half to fill, then tape shut
- coffee can, oatmeal box, ice cream tub, band-aid metal box

NOTES

FUN FOOD

MOM, I'M STARVED!

PEANUT BUTTER AND JELLY COOKIES

1 cup creamy peanut butter
3/4 cup butter or margarine, softened
3 cups all-purpose flour
1/4 cup grape, apple or strawberry jelly

1/3 cup milk
1/2 teaspoon salt
1 1/3 cups sugar
2 teaspoons baking powder

Cream peanut butter, butter and sugar. Stir together dry ingredients, blend into creamed mixture. Beat well. Blend in milk. Shape dough into two 1-1/2-inch rolls 9 inches long; chill for one hour. Slice cookies 1/8 to 1/2-inch thick. Place half of the slices on an ungreased cookie sheet two inches apart. Spread center of each cookie with about 1/2 teaspoon jelly. Cover with remaining slices. Seal edges with tines of a fork. Bake at 350° for 12 to 15 minutes. Cool 1 to 2 minutes; remove from cookie sheet; cool on rack. Makes 3 to 3 1/2 dozen.

ORANGE CREAM FREEZE

1 cup orange juice

2 scoops vanilla ice cream

Put juice and ice cream into a blender. Blend on high speed for 10 seconds. Makes 2 drinks.

THREE CUP TOSS

1 cup chocolate coated candies
1 cup salted peanuts
1 cup raisins

Combine and enjoy!

CRAZY CUBES

Pour any colorful fruit juice or soft drink into an ice cube tray and freeze. Grape, strawberry, orange and like look very pretty. Make in several colors and put one of each color in each glass.

HOMEMADE DRINK BOXES

Use small zip bags and put pieces of an orange in the bag and squeeze juice out of the orange pieces. Open bag, insert straw, zip bag to keep the straw tight.

DO-IT-YOURSELF ICE CREAM SANDWICHES

Spread softened ice cream to the edge of any appropriate cookie (graham crackers are good). Press on top of cookie gently. Wrap or stack in foil or plastic wrap for the freezer.

WATERMELON ON A STICK

Cut watermelon into wedges, put a popsicle stick through the base of the rind. Put them in the freezer until frozen.

BANANA MILK

1 1/2 cups cold milk1 banana

Put milk and banana into a blender. Blend on a high speed for 10 seconds.

APPLE WITCHES

1 applePeanut butter

Wash apple and cut into 3 wedges. Cut out core and seeds. Spread wedges with peanut butter.

PEANUT BUTTER KISSES

2/3 cup instant nonfat dry milk, dry
1/3 cup pancake syrup
1/3 cup peanut butter

Mix together dry milk and syrup until smooth. Stir in peanut butter. Shape into balls. Refrigerate.

EDIBLE PLAYDOUGH

1 cup peanut butter1 1/4 cup powdered sugar
1 cup honey1 1/4 cup powdered milk

In a large bowl mix ingredients thoroughly. Mold anything and everything you wish to create. Then when you get tired of it, eat it! This does store well for several days in the refrigerator.

IRONED SANDWICH

Make up cheese sandwiches as if to grill. Butter the outsides and wrap sandwich in foil. Iron one or two minutes on each side with household iron.

EDIBLE MATCHES

Dip carrot sticks or pretzel sticks in melted chocolate just on one end.

ZOO PARTY MIX

6 cups popped corn
1/4 cup margarine
2 Tablespoons honey
10-oz. package bear-shaped
   graham snacks

1 cup dry roasted peanuts
1/3 cup packed brown sugar
1/2 teaspoon cinnamon
3 pouches of animal-shaped
   chewy fruit

Place popcorn and peanuts in a buttered 15 x 10 x 1-inch baking pan. In a small saucepan combine brown sugar, margarine, honey and cinnamon. Cook and stir over low heat until boiling. Boil gently, uncovered, without stirring, for four minutes. Pour over popcorn and stir to coat. Bake the mixture at 300° for 20 minutes, stirring every 5 minutes. Toss in bear snacks and chewy fruit.

ZOO SANDWICHES

Bread slices
Food coloring

Cream cheese
Cream (1 Tablespoon for 3
   ounces cream cheese)

Put cream cheese and cream into a bowl. Mix until cream cheese is soft. Add food coloring. Cut out bread with cookie cutters. Spread on cream cheese mixture and top as desired. Try honey and peanut butter on wheat bread for bears.

CHILI FRANK BURRITOS

Two 7-inch flour tortillas
Two slices cheese
Two chili-stuffed hot dogs

Wrap tortilla in foil. Heat in a 375° oven for 5 minutes. On top of each tortilla, arrange 1 slice of cheese and 1 hot dog. Fold in ends of tortillas. Roll up tortillas around cheese and hot dogs. Wrap in foil. Bake in oven about 15 minutes or until warm. Makes 2 servings.

BANANA FREEZE SLICES

1/2 package (9 squares) sweet cooking chocolate
2 Tablespoons peanut butter
2 bananas
1 cup crisp rice cereal

Place chocolate in microwave-safe dish. Heat on high for 1 minute. Stir; heat until almost melted, 30 seconds longer. Stir until completely melted. Stir in peanut butter. Dip or roll bananas in chocolate; coating bananas on all sides. Roll bananas in cereal. Freeze until firm, at least 4 hours. Cut banana in half-inch slices before serving. Makes 2 to 4 servings.

MELON RINGS

1 medium cantaloupe or honeydew melon
1 pint strawberries

Cut melon crosswise into rings one-inch thick. Remove seeds. Place slices on individual plates, and with a knife carefully loosen pulp by cutting around the slice 1/4-inch from the rind. Do not remove rind. Slice pulp to make bite-size pieces, leaving rind intact. Rinse strawberries, but do not hull. Arrange in center of melon ring.

MARSHMALLOW PEOPLE

Thread marshmallows on pipe cleaners to form body, arms and legs. Use nuts, candied cherries to make faces; cocoa for hair.

COOKIE MONSTER CANDY

2 cups peanut butter
2 cups honey
2 teaspoons powdered milk
1 teaspoon rolled oats
2 teaspoons mixed raisins and nuts

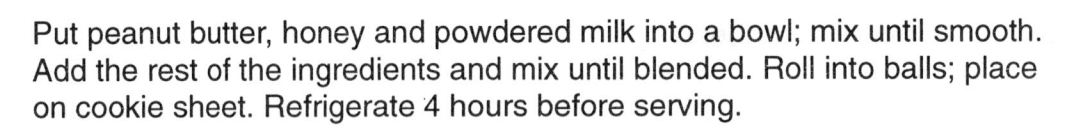

Put peanut butter, honey and powdered milk into a bowl; mix until smooth. Add the rest of the ingredients and mix until blended. Roll into balls; place on cookie sheet. Refrigerate 4 hours before serving.

ZUCCHINI BOAT

Use a zucchini for the base for snacks on a toothpick. Just cut out top of elongated zucchini to resemble a boat. Stick toothpicks into cut-out area.

ORANGE SIPS

Roll an orange between your hands until soft. Use a knife and cut an "X" in the orange. Insert a porous peppermint stick into the "X" and sip away.

RINGS AND DOGS

1 cup macaroni rings
1 pound hot dogs, sliced
10 3/4-ounce can condensed
  tomato soup
1/4 cup chopped onion
2 Tablespoons margarine
1/2 cup water
4 ounces shredded cheese

Cook macaroni until soft as directed on the package. Drain; rinse with hot water. In large skillet, saute hot dogs and onion in margarine until onion is tender. Reduce heat; stir in soup, cheese and water. Cook over low heat, stirring constantly, until cheese is melted. Stir in cooked macaroni.

MAKE YOUR OWN PEANUT BUTTER

1 pound or less of peanuts in the shell

Shell and chop until fine in a blender one cup at-a-time. Add 1 to 2 tablespoons cooking oil. Add salt only if not salted peanuts in the shell. This makes about 1 cup of delicious peanut butter which should be stored in the refrigerator. You can take the easy way out and buy peanuts already shelled.

DIPPED CHIPS

8 ounces semi-sweet chocolate or 1 1/3 cups semi-sweet chocolate chips
2 Tablespoons shortening
7 1/2 ounces can of stacked potato chips

Line cookie sheets with waxed paper. In small saucepan, melt chocolate and shortening over low heat, stirring constantly. Dip chips half way into chocolate; allow excess to drip off. Place on waxed paper-lined cookie sheets; refrigerate to set. Makes 5 to 6 dozen chips.

RAGGEDY ANN SALAD

Body – Fresh or canned peach half
Arms and Legs – Small celery sticks
Head – Half of a hard-cooked egg
Eyes, Nose, Shoes, Buttons – Raisins
Mouth – Piece of a cherry or red hot
Hair – Grated yellow cheese
Skirt – Ruffled leaf lettuce

PEANUT BUTTER BURRITOS

1 package soft tortilla shells

Spread with peanut butter and add any of the following toppings:
    Peanuts, raisins, jelly or jam, small candies, hot fudge sauce,
    (not heated), trail mix, crumbled bacon.
Roll them up and eat.

COOKIE CAT SUNDAES

Place a big scoop of favorite ice cream in a dish. This forms the head. Use color candy-coated milk chocolate candies for eyes and mouth. For ears, push round cookies into the ice cream.

READY TO MAKE SNOW CONES

Freeze orange juice (or any other juice) in ice cube trays or styrofoam egg cartons work great, too. Put frozen cubes in plastic bag to store. To make cones put 3 to 6 cubes at a time in the blender. Turn on and off until it reaches snowy consistency.

TACO PARTY MIX

1/8 cup oleo, melted
Shoe string potatoes
Square-shaped rice cereal

3/4 package taco seasoning
Peanuts
1 can French fried onion rings, broken into pieces

Mix oleo and seasoning; pour over other ingredients. Bake at 350° for 30 to 35 minutes. Stir once after 15 minutes.

MARSHMALLOW DAISIES

For each flower, dip scissors in water. Cut across the flat side of colored miniature marshmallows to form petals. Arrange five petals on wax paper in a daisy design, slightly overlapping tips. Dip inside of flower into colored sugar to coat cut sides of petals.

HARD ROUND TEETHING BISCUITS

2 eggs
1 cup sugar
2-2 1/2 cups flour (white, whole wheat or combination)

Break eggs into a bowl and stir until creamy. Add sugar and continue to stir. Gradually add enough flour to make a stiff dough. Roll out between two sheets of lightly floured waxed paper to about 3/4" thickness. Cut into round shapes. Place on a lightly greased cookie sheet. Let it stand overnight (10-12 hours). Bake at 325° until browned and hard. This will make about 12 durable and almost crumb-free teething biscuits.

CLOWN ICE CREAM CONES

Use cookie for base. Add one scoop ice cream. Put sugar cone on top of ice cream for hat. Make a face on ice cream with candy – chocolate pieces for eyes, red hot for nose, licorice for mouth.

YOGURT POPSICLES

One 3-ounce package gelatin, prepared
  and slightly chilled
1 teaspoon honey
One 8-ounce carton yogurt

Mix together and chill in paper cups. Can put sticks in them or eat with a spoon.

FUDGESICLES

One 4-ounce package regular chocolate pudding mix
3 1/2 cups milk

Prepare as for pudding. Sweeten to taste, if desired. An egg may be added for additional nutritional value. Freeze in molds or paper cups and insert popsicle sticks.

HOMEMADE NOODLES

2 or 3 eggs, whipped and little salt added
3 Tablespoons cream
1+ cups flour

Roll real thin. Let dry awhile and cut with flour on both sides. Can freeze if dry real well.

BARBECUE CUPS

1 pound ground beef
1/2 cup barbecue sauce
1/4 cup chopped onion
1 to 2 Tablespoons brown sugar
10-ounce can refrigerated biscuits
2 ounces shredded Cheddar cheese

Heat oven to 400°. In a large skillet, brown beef, drain. Stir in barbecue sauce, onion and brown sugar; heat until bubbly. Remove from heat; set aside. Separate biscuits into 10 separate biscuits; place each biscuit in ungreased muffin cup. Press dough to cover bottom and sides of cup. Spoon hot meat mixture into cups; sprinkle evenly with cheese. Bake at 400° for 10 to 15 minutes or until crust is golden brown.

CHEESY CHIPS

2 medium baking potatoes
1/2 cup Parmesan cheese
1/2 cup margarine, melted
Salt and pepper to taste

Peel potatoes and slice 1/8-inch thick. Dip slices in melted margarine; then in cheese. Place slices on large baking sheet lined with foil (grease foil with margarine). Sprinkle with salt and pepper. Preheat oven to 375°. Bake 15 to 20 minutes. Makes two servings.

TRAIL MIX

1 cup granola cereal
1/2 cup chopped dates
1/2 cup raisins
1/2 cup salted sunflower kernels
1/2 cup salted roasted soybeans

In a medium bowl, mix cereal, sunflower kernels, soybeans, dates, raisins with a wooden spoon. Store in a jar or a plastic container with a tight lid. Makes 2 1/2 cups.

VEGETABLE PEOPLE

Make vegetable people for a snack. Create with chunks of carrots, celery, potatoes and put together with toothpicks.

PUPPY CHOW FOR PEOPLE

Mix and melt together 1/2 cup margarine, 1 cup peanut butter and 1 large bag of chocolate chips. Pour mixture over 8 cups of crisp square-shaped cereal. Coat well. Put 2 cups powdered sugar in a bag. Dump coated cereal mixture into sugar and shake to coat. Serve or give as a gift in a new clean doggie bowl.

STUFFED CELERY

One 4-ounce can shrimp
1/2 cup mayonnaise
1 Tablespoon chopped onion
2 drops hot pepper sauce
1/4 teaspoon salt
2 Tablespoons lemon juice

Combine and put into celery sticks.

SHRIMP TREE

Insert a styrofoam cone into a styrofoam square and secure. Add endive to the cone with toothpick halves. Start at outside edge of the base and work up. Attach shrimp with toothpicks. Top with a bow.

HONEY APPLE

1 apple
1 popsicle stick
Honey
Nuts and/or toasted wheat germ

Insert stick into the top of an apple. Dip the apple into a bowl of honey, coating evenly. Hold apple over bowl until excess honey has dripped off. Do not rush this step. Roll apple in chopped nuts or toasted wheat germ.

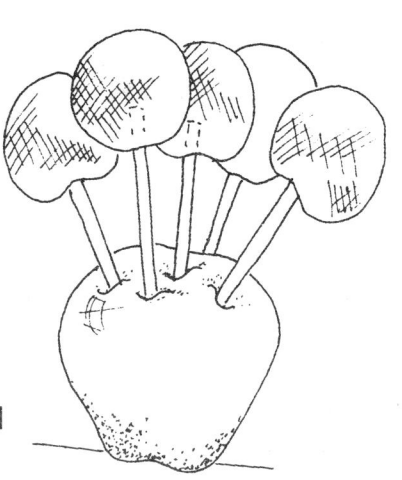

Use apples as a base for table favors. Stick lollipops into an apple and sit around the party table.

PUNCH FOR A PARTY

One 6-ounce can frozen orange juice
One 6-ounce can frozen limeade
One 6-ounce can frozen lemonade
One 12-ounce can apricot nectar
One 12-ounce can pineapple juice
One 2-liter bottle lemon-lime soda of choice

Mix juices according to directions. Add remaining ingredients. To serve, float ice ring with strawberries in punch.

ICE CREAM SNOW

1 cup milk
1/2 cup sugar
1 egg, beaten
1 teaspoon vanilla

Blend the above well and add clean, fresh snow until absorbed.

SWIRL COOKIE POPS

Roll of refrigerated sugar cookie dough
Food coloring
24 wooden sticks

Allow cookie dough to soften at room temperature for 30 minutes. Divide dough into two equal parts. Add 3 or 4 drops of food coloring to half of the dough. Work color into the dough. Roll out colored dough between two sheets of waxed paper to a 12 x 8-inch rectangle. Roll out plain dough in the same manner. Refrigerate dough sheets for 20 minutes. Remove top sheet of waxed paper from both doughs. With plain dough on bottom, place layer of colored dough on top, removing waxed paper. Roll up, jelly-roll fashion, starting with 12-inch side. Wrap tightly in waxed paper. Refrigerate at least one hour. Cut dough into 24 one-half-inch pieces. Place slices on ungreased cookie sheet. Bake at 325° for 10 to 12 minutes.

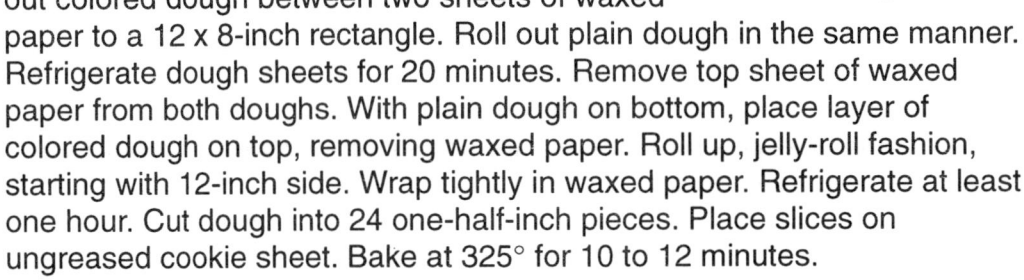

WATERMELON ICE CREAM DESSERT

Mold green sherbet that is softened inside a lettuce keeper. Add pink sherbet that is softened and mini chocolate chips added over green sherbet. Freeze, unmold and slice to look like a slice of watermelon.

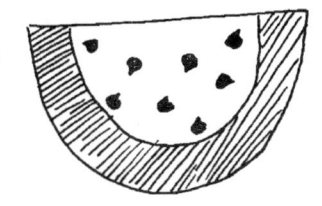

HOT COCOA

1 Tablespoon cocoa
Hot milk

2 Tablespoons sugar
1/8 teaspoon vanilla

Combine cocoa, sugar and salt in a cup. Stir in hot milk to fill the cup. Add vanilla, if desired; stir until blended. One serving.

FRUIT CLOUDS

8 ounces cream cheese, softened
2 teaspoons grated lemon rind
1/2 cup sugar
1 Tablespoon lemon juice

Mix until well blended. Fold in 1 cup heavy cream, whipped. On waxed paper on a cookie sheet spoon mixture to form 10 shells. Freeze until firm. Just before serving, fill with fruit.

ABC SOUP

6 cups chicken broth
2 cups frozen mixed vegetables
1/4 teaspoon thyme leaves
1 cup alphabet macaroni
1/3 cup chopped celery
2 cups cubed, cooked chicken
 or turkey
1 bay leaf
Salt and pepper to taste

In large saucepan, combine broth, chicken, vegetables, celery, onion, thyme and bay leaf. Bring to a boil. Reduce heat and stir in macaroni. Simmer 10 minutes or until macaroni is soft.

CHOCOLATE PEANUT PIZZA

1/2 cup sugar
1/2 cup peanut butter
1/2 teaspoon vanilla
1 1/2 cups flour
1/2 cup packed brown sugar
1/2 cup margarine, softened
1 egg
2 cups miniature marshmallows

Heat oven to 375°. In bowl, combine sugar, brown sugar, margarine, peanut butter, vanilla and egg; blend well. Stir in flour. Press dough evenly over bottom of a 12 or 14-inch pizza pan, forming a rim along the edge. Bake at 375° for 10 minutes. Sprinkle with marshmallows and chocolate chips; continue to bake for 5 to 8 more minutes or until marshmallows are puffy and lightly browned. Cool; cut into wedges.

LEMONADE FLOATS

1 envelope lemonade flavored unsweetened soft drink mix
Ice cubes
1/2 cup water
2 bottles (20 ounces each) ginger ale, chilled
1 pint lemon sherbet

Combine soft drink mix and water in pitcher. Keep chilled. Just before serving, pour about one tablespoon soft drink mixture into ice-filled glasses; fill with ginger ale. Add a scoop of sherbet. Garnish with lemon or lime slices.

PRETZEL ANIMALS

1 package yeast
4 cups flour
1 1/2 cups warm water
1 egg
1 Tablespoon sugar
1 Tablespoon salt

In large bowl mix together yeast, water, sugar and salt. Stir in flour. Knead on table until dough is smooth. Shape dough into animal shapes. Brush with beaten egg. Sprinkle with salt. Bake in oven at 425° for 15 minutes or until golden browned.

STRAWBERRY-LEMONADE PUNCH

2 cans (67 oz.) pink lemonade concentrate
1 can (6 oz.) frozen orange juice concentrate
1 package frozen sliced strawberries
1 bottle ginger ale, chilled

In punch bowl, combine pink lemonade, orange juice, strawberries, 3 cups water. Refrigerate. When ready to use, add ginger ale.

ROOT BEER RED

Fill an ice cube tray with root beer. Add one maraschino cherry to each ice cube section. Freeze. Later, pour more root beer into glasses. Drop two frozen root beer cubes into each glass. Serve at once.

CRUNCH CHEESE SANDWICHES

3 cups rice cereal
4 slices cheese
8 slices bread
2 eggs
1/2 cup milk
1/4 teaspoon salt
3 Tablespoons margarine

Crush cereal. Set aside. Make cheese sandwiches, set aside. In a shallow dish, beat eggs, milk and salt until foamy. Quickly dip cheese sandwiches into egg mixture, then into cereal. Place on well-greased baking sheet. Drizzle with butter. Bake at 450° in oven for 15 minutes or until crisp and golden brown.

BERRY ICE

1 pint fresh berries
3/4 cup sugar or honey
3/4 cup water
1/4 cup orange or lemon juice

Puree fruit in blender. Heat water and sweetener together to a clear syrup and pour into blender. Mix completely. Freeze in plastic containers or as popsicles.

CEREAL LOLLIPOPS

20 marshmallows
2 Tablespoons butter
1/8 teaspoon salt
4 cups round-shaped cereal

Melt marshmallows, butter, and salt over low heat in saucepan. Stir until smooth. Pour mixture over cereal in buttered bowl and mix gently. Shape into ten 2-inch balls. Insert peppermint sticks or other candy sticks into balls. Allow to harden slightly before serving.

BREAD IN A FLOWER POT

Using a regular red clay flower pot, clean thoroughly with hot soapy water and let dry. Butter the interior generously, cover the hole with a small piece of buttered foil. Put plain bread crumbs thoroughly on the interior surface. Make your bread dough (or use frozen loaf) and fill the pot 3/4 full. Oil the top of the dough, cover with a towel and set in a warm place to double in size. Heat oven to 350° and bake the bread for 30 minutes in a large pot, 15 minutes in a small pot. The bread cooks quickly because of the additional heat from the clay pot. Leave the bread in the pot for 15 minutes to cool before lifting out to cool. Decorate the pot with ribbon and bow. Set the bread back into the pot when cooled and seal with cellophane.

ICE CREAM SANDWICHES

Slice refrigerator cookie dough and bake as directed. When cool, put one scoop of ice cream between two cookies.

DO-IT-YOURSELF SUNDAES

Have several flavors of ice cream or yogurt available as well as some of the following toppings:

NUTS – peanuts, walnuts, cashews
SAUCES – honey, maple syrup, chocolate syrup, strawberry syrup, butterscotch
FRUITS – chopped dates, apricots, berries, sliced bananas, pineapple, cherries, peaches
GOODIES – chocolate chips, granola, coconut, toasted wheat germ, whipped cream, candy sprinkles, broken candy bar pieces, bubble gum

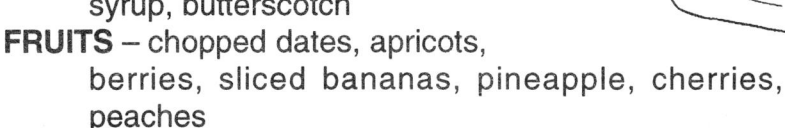

Ice cream stores will usually sell you banana split boats for a very reasonable price to add more character to your party.

Scoop several flavors of ice cream into balls and freeze on wax paper in a shallow pan, cover. They will be waiting for your assembly when the dessert is to be served. Serve in various pitchers or sauce boats with ladles.

Arrange garnishes and toppings in individual bowls. Include coconut, chopped nuts, granola, maraschino cherries and whipped cream – all prepared ahead, covered and refrigerated. Include serving utensil with each.

To serve, arrange frozen ice cream balls in a large bowl. Set out sauces, garnishes, dessert dishes, napkins and spoons. Let everyone create their own dessert. It will save you time and guests will enjoy it! Great for a child's party at school or at home. You can make your sundae bar as simple or as lavish as you prefer.

Try one of these ice cream sundae sauces or place the ice cream toppings in an attractive container and give as a gift with the recipe included.

PRALINE – Melt 1/4 cup butter in a small saucepan. Stir in one cup packed brown sugar and 1/2 cup heavy cream until sugar is dissolved. Add 1/2 cup light corn syrup. Cook and stir until sauce thickens. Stir in 3/4 cup chopped pecans and 1 teaspoon vanilla. Serve warm.

BLUEBERRY MARSHMALLOW – Puree two cups of fresh or frozen blueberries. Fold into 1/2 cup marshmallow cream.

RAISIN-WALNUT – Soak 1 cup raisins in 1 cup hot water for five minutes, drain. Stir in 1 cup maple-flavored syrup and 1 cup walnut pieces.

ORANGE SAUCE – Stir six ounces thawed frozen orange juice concentrate, one tablespoon brown sugar and 1/2 teaspoon ginger until sugar dissolves.

RUM-APPLE – Saute two cups chopped apples in 1/4 cup butter until crisp and tender. Stir in 1/4 cup packed brown sugar and 1/4 cup water; cook five minutes. Stir in 1/2 teaspoon rum extract.

PEPPERMINT – Whip 1 cup heavy cream until frothy; gradually beat in one tablespoon sugar, 1/2 teaspoon vanilla and 3 tablespoons crushed hard peppermint candies until soft peaks form.

HOT FUDGE – Blend together 1 1/2 cups sugar, 4 tablespoons flour and 2 tablespoons cocoa in medium-sized bowl. Bring 1 1/2 cups water to boil in medium-sized pan. Add sugar mixture and stir until smooth. Add 1/4 cup margarine; simmer over low heat for 15 to 20 minutes. Add 1 teaspoon vanilla.

APPLE-CARAMEL – Mix together 8 ounces cream cheese, 1/4 cup brown sugar, 1/4 teaspoon vanilla and 1 jar caramel topping. Chop up apple and add to mixture.

TURN ORDINARY FOOD INTO SOMETHING SPECIAL

- **Freeze grapes** and then add to drinks.
- Serve **cooked peas** in a scooped out tomato.
- Call slices of cucumbers, **"cucumber coins".**
- Insert a popsicle stick in the end of a **hot dog** and microwave.
- Make **swords** by putting banana slices, cheese slices etc. into thin pretzel sticks.
- Fill **mushroom caps** with carrots and/or peas.
- Cut **jelled cranberry sauce** into various holiday shapes for garnishes.
- Cut **acorn squash** in half and remove seeds and membrane. Bake, then fill with buttered peas and top with strips of grilled bacon.
- Custard cups, muffin pans, ice cube trays, and empty tin cans make good **salad molds**.
- Place **peach halves** upside down in greens on a salad tray – fill with raspberry jam, cottage cheese or just accent with cloves.
- Serve **fruit salad** in hollowed-out pineapple half
- Make **"wreath" pancakes** and serve with strawberry syrup.
- For a **"satellite" garnish** clean and cut carrot sticks 1/4-inch thick and three-inches long. Thread each carrot stick through a pitted ripe olive.
- Cut bread with a **cookie cutter** for toast and add raisins for eyes.
- Use pointed paper cups for making gelatin **"trees"** – cut away paper when mold is firm and decorate with cream cheese.
- Fill cooked **onion cups** with hot baked beans.
- Hollow out **unsliced bread** to serve dips in.
- Fill **orange cups** with frosted grapes as a garnish on meat trays.
- Cut hard-boiled **egg whites** into stars, crescents or other shapes to use on the border of food trays.

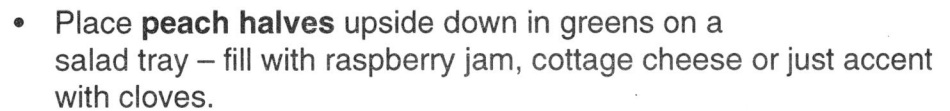

- Cut **candied cherry into petal shapes** and arrange in the shape of holly on top of whipped cream or fruit slices to garnish.

- Put a string through **sugared fruit slices** with a needle and hang them on the tree.

- Hang a **candy cane over the edge of a cup** or glass to make that holiday drink special.

- Before you bake **Christmas cookies** make a hole in the top of them so you can hang them on the tree with a string or ribbon. (A straw works.)

- Add **red and green gumdrops** to your popcorn and cranberry garlands for the Christmas tree. With a straight pin, attach a piece of popcorn, cranberry or gumdrop to the top of each branch to carry out your theme.

- Make **spice balls** by pushing cloves into an orange. Put ribbon on the orange and anchor the ribbon with cloves so it will not slip.

- **Small apples** with sturdy stems can be decorated with sequins held on with straight pins for decorations. Tie ribbon to the stem.

- Create a **gelatin Christmas tree** by hardening lime gelatin in individual paper cups. When turned upside down these will resemble a tree.

- Make **cookie place cards**. You will need two cut-out cookies for each place card. Decorate and write the name on one cookie using melted chocolate or icing. Place a dab of chocolate or icing in the middle of other cookie and stand decorated cookie in it while propping it against something until it dries.

- Cut off the top of an orange and scoop out the inside – put in **orange sherbet** and freeze until ready to serve.

- Place one scoop of ice cream in a **shortcake** – top as desired.

- Serve **ice cream in five-ounce plastic cups** – decorate with paint pens, bows, etc. before filling.

- Bake **muffins in nut cups** for variety – leave in nut cups for serving.

- Hollow out **citrus fruit** to make a "basket" to serve jams and jellies in for brunch.

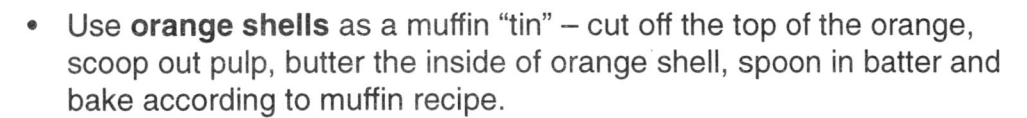

- Use **orange shells** as a muffin "tin" – cut off the top of the orange, scoop out pulp, butter the inside of orange shell, spoon in batter and bake according to muffin recipe.

- Serve **soup** in soup bowls lined with warmed tortilla shells.

- Serve various berries in a **mother-of-pearl abalone shell**.

- For **frosted grapes** wash grapes, leave in a big bunch and roll in dry, green gelatin and chill.

- Stack **petit fours** in shape of Christmas tree for holiday party.

- For napkin rings use **fresh ivy**.

- Tie bows around **stemmed glasses** for holidays.

- **Decorate candles and candleholders** with icing for holidays – will wash off, sprinkle icing with glitter, sprinkles, etc.

- For **Mexican theme**, serve food in pottery pieces and ice cream in crisp tortilla shells.

- Garnish your **meat tray** by hollowing out small cooked beets – fill with horseradish, mustard, mayonnaise.

- Use miniature muffin tins or styrofoam egg cartons to mold.

- Put **cupcake stick decorations** into sandwich when serving for special occasion – flag, baseball, etc.

- To add color and dimension to your fruit or **sandwich tray**, cut four thin slices of cantaloupe with the skin on, turn upside down and prop onto bowl of dip in the center of the tray,

- To make **orange cubes** as a change to serve with coffee, rub a regular lump of sugar over an unpeeled, slightly scraped orange and sprinkle with grated orange rind.

- Cut **green or red peppers** in half, remove the membrane and seeds. Fill with vegetables for each serving such as cauliflower with cheese sauce.

- Make **unusual ice cubes** by placing fresh berries, maraschino cherries, lemon or orange wedges in the ice tray and then fill the tray with colored water or fruit juice.

- Using your favorite **popcorn ball recipe** or cereal mixture, turn them into a wreath, jack-o-lantern, bunny, pumpkin, etc.

- Use **cookie cutter to cut bread** in shapes for party sandwiches. Spread with peanut butter, cream cheese, jelly, chicken or ham salad, etc.

DECORATING CAKES, CUPCAKES

Fasten **gumdrop flowers** onto tops of cupcakes and cakes with light corn syrup.

Bake your favorite brownies in flat bottom ice cream cones. After baking, dip in melted chocolate and add candy sprinkles.

Top cupcakes with animal crackers, gum drops, tiny colored marshmallows.

For a **clown face** use chocolate pieces for eyes, red hot for nose and licorice for the mouth.

Edible **decorating "glue"** can be made with a thin coating of honey, then add shredded coconut, toasted wheat germ.

To make **gumdrop flowers** roll gumdrops between 2 sheets of waxed paper. Cut into petals and leaves and arrange on cake in the shape of flowers.

Icing can be squeezed from small plastic bag with one corner cut out.

Moisten the top of a peppermint candy, sit three red lifesavers on top of the candy. Insert a small candle in the lifesavers.

Add **candle rings** to your cupcakes by placing a hard circular piece of candy in the middle and then add a candle.

For **natural frosting colorings** add a bit of cranberry juice for pink; carrot juice for yellow/orange; grape juice concentrate for a dark pink; crushed blueberries for blue.

To **accent a tube cake**, roll grapes in water and then in powdered sugar. Group around cake on plate. Can put small amount of icing or whipped cream to hold in place.

Melt a small amount of chocolate chips to use as **"paint"** for names and greetings with a clean watercolor brush. Names, etc. can be painted from the melted chocolate onto waxed paper and removed when it hardens.

An unusual effect for a cake is a **wishbone cake**. Spray paint several chicken wishbones with gold spray paint. Arrange them around the edge of a frosted cake so the wishbones extend to the top and sides.

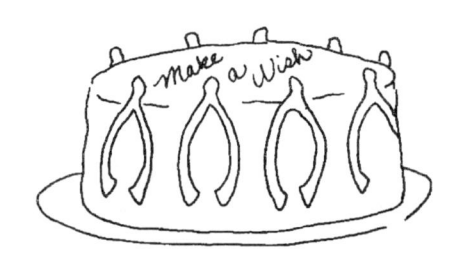

Make **chocolate flowers** by melting two squares of semisweet chocolate over low heat. Cool slightly; spread 1/8-inch thick on waxed paper. Refrigerate for 10 minutes. Cut into flowers, stems and/or leaves. Keep refrigerated until ready to use.

Tasty **orange icing** can be made by substituting orange juice for the water or milk. Two cups of confectioners sugar, 3 tablespoons margarine, softened and 2 tablespoons orange juice. Beat.

Turn a white cake mix into a **rainbow cake**. Make the mix as directed. Divide mixture into five bowls. Add a different food color to each bowl of mix. Stir well. Pour mixtures one-at-a time on top of each other into greased tube pan. Bake as directed.

Children love **"money cakes"**. Make batter as usual. Before baking, wrap various coins in aluminum foil and put into batter. Children love to find the coins in their cake. Must supervise! Peg Berry has pleased children for years with this cake.

PARTY TRAIN CAKE

Spread frosting on a cardboard cake board in a 17-inch long, "S" shape to resemble a train track. Put sprinkles on icing. Use frozen snack size cakes or bake into small cake sizes. Arrange the train cars onto the track. Frost each a different color, add peppermint candies for wheels, etc.

DIRT CAKE

Two 3-ounce packages of instant pudding
Mix with 3 cups milk. Mix until thick.
CREAM: 8 ounces cream   1 1/2 sticks margarine
         1 cup powdered sugar
Fold in with pudding. Fold in 8 ounces whipped topping. Put 3/4 to 1 pound chocolate sandwich cookies in blender or roll to crush. Put into a clean flower pot that is new. Alternate cookies and pudding mixtures to resemble a potted plant. Start with cookies and end with cookies. Add gummy worms on the top. Can also make into individual servings in clear plastic cups.

PITTER PATTER OF LITTLE CAKES

Prepare cake as desired. Freeze cake for one hour before cutting. Cut cake into pieces using a foot-shaped pattern. Ice and trim with icing around the shape of a foot.

GRADUATION CAP CUPCAKES

Make 12 yellow cupcakes.
Chocolate icing
12 squares of chocolate covered graham cracker cookies
4 2/3 yards white yarn
12 dark brown candy-coated chocolates

To make each cap, place a cupcake upside down and frost sides and top with chocolate icing, reserving 2 tablespoons. Place a graham cracker square on top of each cupcake.

To make tassel, cut the yarn into 24 seven-inch lengths. Holding two lengths together, fold them in half and tie a knot about 1/2-inch from the fold to form a loop. Repeat with remaining yard to form 12 tassels.

Place a little chocolate icing in the center of each graham cracker cookie. Center the loop of a tassel on top of each cupcake and lightly press a candy-coated chocolate over each tassel to look like a button.

BROWNIE CUPCAKES

4 oz. semi-sweet chocolate squares
2 sticks margarine
1 large package chopped pecans
4 large unbeaten eggs
1 cup flour
1 3/4 cup sugar
1 teaspoon salt

Mix all ingredients but do not beat. Place in cupcake pan and bake at 325° for 25 minutes.

CUPCAKES FOR EVERY MONTH OF THE YEAR

Kids love 'em, grown-ups love 'em! This hand held treat is good especially when serving a large group. Cupcakes are easy to transport, easy to serve and easy to eat!

JANUARY – "SNOWMAN CUPCAKE"

1 white frosted cupcake
2 large marshmallows
2 small marshmallows
2 toothpicks
12 mini chocolate morsels

Push one toothpick into the center of two large marshmallows, insert into the top of a frosted cupcake. Break remaining toothpick in half and use as arms. Place small marshmallows on the end of "arms" for hands. Decorate snowman using mini chocolate morsels for the eyes, nose, mouth and buttons. A small amount of frosting will "glue" them onto marshmallows. Remove toothpicks before eating.

FEBRUARY – "CHEERY CHERRIES"

Press a small candle into the hole of the stem end of a maraschino cherry. Place on a frosting cupcake.

MARCH – "SHAMROCK SALUTE"

Cut out green fruit flavored gelatin with a shamrock cookie cutter. Place gelatin on the top of a frosted cupcake.

APRIL – "EASTER BASKETS"

To make cupcakes that look like Easter baskets, use 1/2 of a pipe cleaner and stick into the cupcake for a handle. Ice the cupcake and then add green colored coconut on the icing to resemble Easter grass. Top with 3 small jelly beans.

MAY – "GUMDROP FLOWERS"

Roll gumdrops between two sheets of waxed paper. Cut into petals and leaves and then arrange on top of cupcakes. Now add a pipe cleaner for handle and add ribbon to look like a basket of flowers.

JUNE – "CARNIVAL CAKE"

Place an animal cracker on top of an iced cupcake. Can dip the animal cracker in melted semi-sweet chocolate, if desired.

JULY – "FOURTH OF JULY CUPCAKES"

Frost cupcake with white icing. Top with several small red candles which will resemble firecrackers when lit.

AUGUST – "SCHOOL DAYS"

Frost cupcake as desired. Then write "ABC" on the top with icing or cut the letters out of fruit leather.

SEPTEMBER – "APPLES FOR TEACHER"

Add 1 or 2 drops only of red food coloring to white frosting. Frost cupcakes with pink frosting. Cut stem of each maraschino cherry so that it is only about 1/2-inch long. Place one on each cupcake.

OCTOBER – "HALLOWEEN CATS"

Add 1 or 2 drops of red and 1 or 2 drops of yellow food coloring to white frosting. Frost cupcakes with the orange frosting. Slice a 1-inch black gumdrop into 3 pieces horizontally. Use small rounded end slice for head; use largest slice for body. Cut ears and tail from third slice. Form a cat on cupcake with gumdrop pieces.

NOVEMBER – "PUMPKINS"

Frost cupcakes with white icing. To make each pumpkin cut a small slip in top of a 1-inch orange gumdrop. Stick a small piece of a green gumdrop in slit for stem.

DECEMBER – "HOLIDAY SURPRISE"

Add a cherry, nuts, chocolate, mincemeat, cream cheese or any goody you want to surprise with in the middle of cupcake batter before baking. Top cupcake with a flower petal by placing a small candle in the center of a circle of five colored mini marshmallows.

"SANTA CLAUS CUPCAKES"

Mix and bake cupcakes as directed. Divide icing into three separate bowls. In the first bowl add 3 or 4 drops of red food coloring to white icing to make a deep red icing for Santa's hat. In the second bowl mix 1 drop of red and 1 drop of yellow for the flesh color. Leave the third bowl white.

Cover the top of the cupcake with a thin layer of the flesh colored icing. Then spread the top half with red icing for the hat. Use silver decorating balls for the eyes. Use a decorating tube to add he beard, eyebrows, moustache and white for the hat.

"FROSTY CUPCAKES"

Combine 1 cup sour cream with 1/4 cup powdered sugar. Stir in 16 ounces frozen strawberries and 8 ounces crushed pineapple, undrained. Pour into cupcake liners. Remove from freezer 10 minutes before serving.

BREAKFAST FUN

BREAKFAST-ON-THE-GO

Cut the pita bread in half and fill with various items of choice – scrambled eggs and ham, cereal, cottage cheese and fruit. Makes a great on-the-go breakfast to hold and eat in the car.

BREAKFAST ICE CREAM CONE

Fill an ice cream cone with low-fat yogurt. Add sliced bananas, strawberries, raisins or other fruit. Sprinkle on a topping of crushed cereal.

BREAKFAST PIZZA

1 pound bulk sausage
1 pkg. (8) crescent rolls
1 cup frozen hash browns, thawed
1 cup shredded sharp cheese
2 tablespoons Parmesan cheese

6 eggs
1/4 cup milk
1/4 teaspoon pepper
1/2 teaspoon salt

Cook sausage until brown; drain. Separate crescent rolls and place in ungreased 12-inch pizza pan or 9 x 13-inch pan. Press together and up the sides; seal. Spoon sausage over the crust. Sprinkle on potatoes and top with cheese. Put this part in refrigerator overnight. Then beat eggs, milk and seasonings; pour over crust. Sprinkle with Parmesan cheese. Bake at 375° for 25 to 30 minutes. Serves 6 or 8.

INITIAL PANCAKES

Make pancake batter as directed. With a small amount of batter in a teaspoon, draw each child's initial backwards on a hot griddle. Brown about one minute, pour more batter over the initial to form a pancake. Bake until bubbles appear, turn and bake as for regular pancakes.

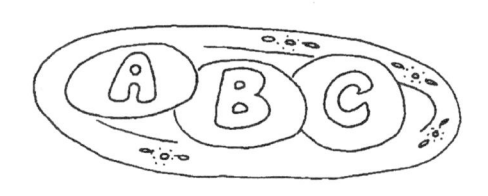

DONUTS

Use refrigerated biscuit dough. Punch a hole in the middle of each biscuit (a bottle cap will be the right size). Fry in one-inch of hot oil for about one minute or until lightly brown on both sides. Fry the "holes" too. When you remove from oil, shake in a bag of cinnamon and sugar or powdered sugar.

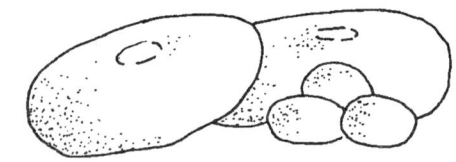

APPLE RINGS

Slice firm, unpeeled apples 1/4-inch thick and dust with flour. Heat enough butter in a skillet to cover the bottom, add apple rings and cook turning frequently until golden brown and tender. Top apple rings with cooked sausage patty.

BUTTERFLY PANCAKES

Bake pancakes as directed. To serve, cut pancakes through the center. Place curved sides together to look like butterfly wings. Place a hot, browned sausage link in the center.

FRAMED EGG

Use a round cookie cutter to cut a hole in the center of a slice of bread. Save the center for bread crumbs. Break an egg into a small cup. Put about 2 tablespoons butter into a 6-inch skillet. Put bread into skillet. Cook about two minutes or until bottom is golden. Turn over with pancake turner. Carefully slide egg into hole in bread and sprinkle egg with salt and pepper, if desired. Cover skillet and cook 3 to 5 minutes or until egg is done. Use pancake turner to lift egg out. One serving.

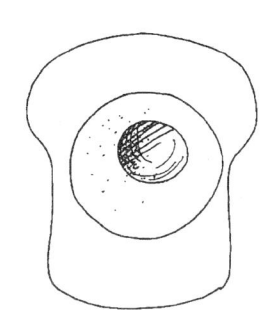

CINNAMON TWISTERS

1 tube refrigerated buttermilk biscuits
1/3 cup melted butter
1/3 cup sugar
1 1/4 teaspoon cinnamon

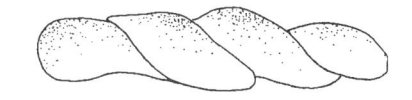

Flatten each biscuit and stretch it into a narrow shape. Dip into the melted butter, then the sugar and cinnamon. Twist and place on a greased cookie sheet. Bake as biscuit directs.

ORANGE FRENCH TOAST

2 eggs
1/4 teaspoon salt
2/3 cup orange juice

3/4 cup dry fine bread crumbs
8 slices of bread

Beat together eggs, salt and orange juice. Dip bread slices into mixture, then into bread crumbs, coating evenly on both sides. Brown bread on both sides on greased, hot griddle.

SYRUP: 1 cup light corn syrup
        1 teaspoon orange rind, grated
        1/4 cup orange juice
Simmer five minutes and serve over French toast.

EGGS IN BOLOGNA CUPS

2 teaspoons shortening
6 slices bologna, each about four inches across
6 eggs
6 teaspoons milk
Salt
Pepper
Paprika

Heat oven to 375°. Grease six muffin cups with some shortening using pastry brush. Melt two teaspoons shortening in skillet over low heat. Place three slices bologna in the skillet and fry until the edges curl and the centers puff. Lift each slice with tongs into a muffin cup and press down so the slice fits the cup. Repeat with remaining bologna slices. Break one egg into the center of each bologna slice to hold it down. Pour 1 teaspoon milk over each egg. Sprinkle eggs lightly with salt, pepper and paprika. Bake uncovered in 375° oven for 15 to 20 minutes or until the eggs are set. Loosen each bologna cup with knife and lift to platter with spoon.

ORANGE JUICE DELIGHT

1 can (6 oz.) frozen orange juice concentrate
1 cup milk
1 cup water
1/2 cup sugar
1/2 teaspoon vanilla
2 ice cubes

Blend in blender until smooth and serve.

BACON BUTTER

In small mixing bowl, cream together 1/2 cup butter or margarine and 3/4 teaspoon prepared mustard. Blend in 4 slices crisp-cooked and crumbled bacon.

BREAKFAST TACOS

1 cup hash brown potato mix with onions found in refrigerator section of supermarket
2 cups hot water
3/4 teaspoon salt
8 flour tortillas
6 eggs, well beaten
1/2 pound bulk pork sausage, cooked, crumbled and drained
1/2 teaspoon salt
Pepper to taste
2 tablespoons butter or margarine
Picante sauce (optional)

Combine hash browns, water and 3/4 teaspoon salt; mix well. Let stand 15 minutes, uncovered. Drain hash browns. Wrap tortillas securely in aluminum foil; bake at 350° for 10 minutes or until thoroughly heated. Combine hash browns, eggs, sausage, 1/2 teaspoon salt and pepper; mix well. Melt butter in a large skillet, cook over low heat until eggs are done. Spoon mixture into tortillas. Fold tortillas in half, add picante sauce, if desired.

APPLE TURNOVERS

8 oz. package crescent rolls
2 large cooking apples, cut into slices
2 tablespoons margarine, melted
1/4 to 1/2 cup sugar
1 teaspoon cinnamon
1/4 cup orange juice

Preheat oven to 400°. Unroll and separate rolls. Cut in half lengthwise to make 16 triangles. Place apple slices on dough and roll up. Arrange in lightly greased 9 x 13-inch pan. Drizzle with butter. Combine sugar and cinnamon and sprinkle over rolls. Pour orange juice into pan but not directly over the rolls. Bake 20 minutes.

PEANUT BUTTER PANCAKES WITH JELLY SYRUP

1 cup complete pancake mix
1 cup water
1/2 cup creamy peanut butter
1/2 to 1 cup favorite jelly

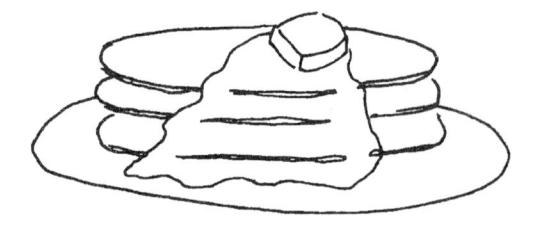

Heat griddle to 350°. In small bowl, combine all ingredients except jelly; beat at medium speed, just until blended. If batter is too thick, stir in 1/2 tablespoon additional water. Lightly grease the griddle.

When griddle is heated pour batter onto hot griddle forming pancakes. Turn when edges begin to brown and bubbles break on the surface. In small saucepan, heat jelly, stirring frequently until smooth. Serve jelly over pancakes.

BREAKFAST PIGS-IN-BLANKET

Use refrigerator biscuits and miniature sausage links. Cut biscuit in half and wrap around the precooked sausage link. Bake until biscuit is brown.

EGG SAILBOATS

1 dozen eggs, hard-cooked
1/2 cup mayonnaise
1 teaspoon mustard
2 dozen toothpicks
1 sheet paper

Shell eggs, slice in half and remove yolks.
Combine yolks with mayonnaise and mustard and return a spoonful of mixture to hollow of each egg white. Tape small paper triangles to toothpicks and stick them in egg halves prior to serving.

HOLIDAY FOODS

GEORGE WASHINGTON CHERRY NUT COOKIES

1 package (18 1/2 oz.) white cake mix
1/2 cup oil
2 eggs
1 1/2 cups thawed frozen red tart cherries, drained
1/2 cup chopped walnuts

Combine cake mix, oil and eggs. Mix at low speed until blended (batter will be very thick). Stir in cherries and nuts. Drop by the teaspoonful onto greased baking sheet. Bake at 350° for 10 to 12 minutes. Cool on baking sheet about one minute. Remove to wire racks to cool. Cookies may be stored in refrigerator in a covered container up to one week.

GEORGE WASHINGTON'S CHERRY VANILLA FREEZE

8 maraschino cherries
1 package instant vanilla pudding (3 oz.)
2 cups milk

Cut each cherry in half. Make the pudding according to the package directions, using the milk. Stir in the cherries. Fill four dessert dishes and place in the freezer for one hour.

**SUCCESS is getting what you want;
HAPPINESS is wanting what you get!**

The first sign of spring is the celebration of Valentine's Day. It is a day to make good use of your heart-shaped cookie cutter . . . for toast, cheese, jello and cookies. Cut heart shapes from bread and then spread with sandwich spread.

STRAWBERRY COOKIES

1 can sweetened condensed milk
1 cup flaked coconut
1 Tablespoons sugar
3/4 pound almonds, ground
1/2 teaspoon almond extract
1/2 teaspoon vanilla extract
6 ounces strawberry gelatin (reserve 1/4 package)

Mix well. Let stand in refrigerator for one hour. Shape into strawberries. Roll in the remaining gelatin. Make powdered sugar icing. Tint green for stems. DO NOT BAKE.

HEART PRETZELS

Make pretzels into the shape of hearts.

RED RASPBERRY RAUSER

10-ounce package frozen raspberries, thawed
8-ounce carton raspberry yogurt
1/3 cup chilled pineapple juice

Place all ingredients in blender. Cover, blend on medium-low speed for 30 seconds until smooth and thick. Pour into glasses. Makes five 1/2-cup servings.

SNOWBALL CAKE

2 Tablespoons unflavored gelatin
1 cup orange juice
1 teaspoon lemon juice
1/2 cup granulated sugar
Dash salt
4 cups whipped topping
1 angel food cake ring
1/4 cup flaked coconut

Line a medium bowl with waxed paper. In a separate bowl, mix together gelatin and 4 tablespoons cold water, until dissolved. Add 1 cup boiling water, orange juice, lemon juice, sugar and salt. Mix and chill until syrupy. Add 3 cups whipped topping to chilled gelatin. Break angel food cake into bite-sized cubes. Fold cake into gelatin mix. Pour into lined bowl. Chill until firm. Turn out onto plate, frost with remaining topping and coconut. Serves 15.

STRAWBERRY WHIPPED CREAM ICING

10-ounce package frozen strawberries
1 package plain gelatin
    (soften in 1/4 cup cold water)
Pinch of salt
1/4 cup sugar
1 pint whipped cream
Red food coloring
Angel food cake

Thaw strawberries, drain and heat juice with sugar, salt and gelatin until dissolved; cool slightly. Mash strawberries with a fork; add to gelatin mixture. Whip cream until stiff, fold into strawberry mixture. Add a few drops of food coloring for desired shade of pink. Allow icing to firm up for 5 to 10 minutes. Slice angel food cake into three layers. Ice with frosting and store in refrigerator.

LOLLIPOP VALENTINES

12 popsicle sticks
1/2 cup semisweet morsels
1/3 cup light brown sugar
1 large egg
1/4 cup unsweetened cocoa powder

2 cups all-purpose flour
1/2 cup butter, softened
1/2 teaspoon vanilla
1/4 teaspoon salt

Soak popsicle sticks in a bowl of cold water for one hour. In heavy saucepan, stir chocolate chips until melted over very low heat. Remove from heat; let cool. With an electric mixer combine butter, brown sugar, vanilla until fluffy. Beat in egg and chocolate. Add flour, cocoa powder and salt. Divide dough in half. Roll each half out to 1/8-inch thickness between two sheets of waxed paper. Freeze in waxed paper for five minutes. Peel top sheets of waxed paper off dough, cut dough out using 3-inch heart-shaped cutter. Reroll scraps; freeze again 5 minutes, cut out. Place half of heart one-inch apart on cookie sheet. Drain popsicle sticks; pat dry. Place one stick on each heart to make 2 1/2-inch handle, pressing lightly into dough. Place remaining hearts on top; press edges gently to seal. Bake for 10 minutes at 375°. Cool and then decorate as desired.
as desired.

IRISH MULLIGAN STEW

2 pounds beef stew meat
2 large carrots, cut in chunks
1 large onion, thickly sliced
2 medium potatoes, quartered
1/2 package frozen peas
1 teaspoon salt
1/8 teaspoon pepper
1 can condensed cream of mushroom or tomato soup

Combine all ingredients in a large casserole. Cover tightly with lid. Bake at 300° for 3 hours or until the meat is tender. May be served with soda biscuits or any type of warm bread.

BISCUITS

4 cups self-rising flour
1 cup vegetable shortening

2 cups buttermilk

Mix together. Roll out on floured board and cut out with biscuit cutter. Bake at 400° until brown.

ST. PATRICK'S PIE

1-3 ounce package vanilla pudding mix (not instant)
1-3 ounce package lime gelatin
2 cups water
1 envelope whipped topping mix
1 baked 9-inch pie crust, graham cracker

Combine pie mix, gelatin and water in saucepan. Cook and stir until thick and clear; chill until mixture begins to set. Prepare whipped topping mix; reserve 1/3 cup for garnish. Blend remainder of whipped topping into chilled pudding mixture. Top pie with reserved whipped topping. Form shamrocks from green cherries for garnish.

EASTER CAKE

Make 3 round cake layers. When cool, stack all 3 on top of each other having cut the center out of the top layer only. Fill the cut-out area with coconut and candy Easter eggs. Add a handle made from rolled-up aluminum foil, pipe cleaners or whatever you desire.

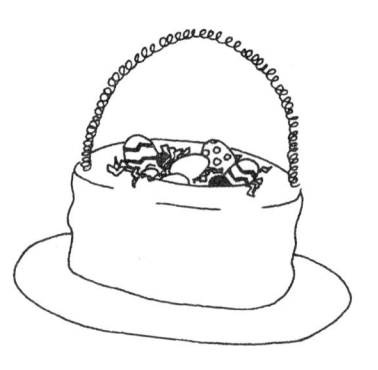

TINTING COCONUT

Add a few drops of food coloring into a small amount of water in a bowl, and add coconut and toss with a fork until evenly distributed or toss in a small jar 1 1/2 cups of coconut with 1 to 2 tablespoons fruit flavored gelatin and shake well.

BUNNY SALAD

Place a canned pear half on a bed of lettuce. Add raisins for eyes, a strawberry attached with a toothpick for a nose. Toothpicks for whiskers and cheese (or paper) for the ears.

EGG YOLK PAINT

Combine 1/4 teaspoon water with one egg yolk. Divide among several small dishes and put different food coloring into each dish. Paint designs on cookies before baking.

BUNNY CAKE

Bake two round cake layers. Leave one layer round. Cut the other layer as shown. Dye coconut pink for inside ears. Decorate face with jelly beans, licorice, chocolate chips, raisins, etc.

EGG-SHAPED COOKIES

Make an egg-shaped cookie cutter by bending and shaping the open end of a 6-ounce juice can. Decorate with choice of icings or decorations.

NEST SALAD

Grated carrot   Mayonnaise
Chinese noodles   Peas or grapes

Mix grated carrot with Chinese noodles and enough mayonnaise to moisten. Put a mound of this on the plate and push in the middle with a spoon to form a nest. Peas or grapes can be used to resemble eggs.

BUNNY ICE CREAM

Lay 3 balls of ice cream on a plate in a row. Use a large one in the center, medium size for the head and small one for the tail. Cover with shredded coconut. Use jelly beans or almonds for the eyes and nose; cut paper for the ears and licorice for whiskers.

CHOCOLATE CHICKS AND BUNNIES

One 6-oz. package chocolate chips
One tablespoon shortening
Tiny colored candies

Cover cookie sheet with waxed paper. Heat the chocolate chips and one tablespoon shortening in saucepan over low heat until chips are melted. Spread the chocolate mixture in a six-inch square pan about 1/4-inch thick on the waxed paper. Sprinkle generously with candies. Refrigerate about 1 minute. Cut out chocolate figures with a cookie cutter. Refrigerate 30 minutes or until firm. Can use bunnies or chicks to decorate a cake or cupcakes. Perhaps stick them on a graham cracker with a little icing.

BUNNY BISCUITS

Using refrigerated biscuits, cut one in half horizontally, then cut one of those pieces in half to use as the head. Cut the remaining piece in half for ears. Pinch out a bit for the tail. Bake as directed.

NESTS

1 can (16 1/2 oz.) frosting
4 cups chow mein noodles
Small jelly beans

Cover cookie sheet with waxed paper. Heat frosting in saucepan over low heat until frosting is liquid, stirring constantly. Remove from heat. Stir in 4 cups chow mein noodles until coated. Drop the mixture by 1/4 cupfuls about one inch apart onto the waxed paper. Make a hollow in the center of each, using the back of a spoon. Fill with jelly beans.

FOURTH OF JULY SALAD

1st Layer: Two 3-oz. packages red raspberry gelatin
3 cups hot water
Dissolve gelatin in hot water, pour in a 9 x 13-inch pan and let set.

2nd Layer: One 3-oz. package unflavored gelatin
1/2 cup cold water   1 cup sugar
1/2 cup nuts   2 teaspoons vanilla
1 cup milk   8 oz. cream cheese

Soften gelatin in cold water. Heat milk. Add sugar, gelatin mixture and vanilla. Blend in cream cheese mixture until smooth. Add nuts. Pour over first layer. Let set.

3rd Layer: One 3-oz. package raspberry gelatin
1 cup hot water
One No. 3 can blueberries, undrained

Dissolve gelatin in hot water. Add undrained blueberries. When partially set, pour over second layer and refrigerate.

FOURTH OF JULY CAKE

Bake cake as desired. Frost with white frosting or non-dairy whipped topping. Decorate top of cake as a flag. Arrange blueberries in a square in upper left-hand corner of cake. Make strips across the cake with sliced strawberries with white topping showing through the stripes.

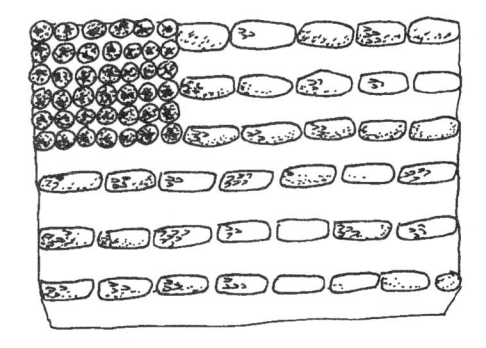

HALLOWEEN

HALLOWEEN BAGEL SPREAD

Mix 1/4 cup pumpkin with 8 ounces softened cream cheese for a Halloween bagel spread.

PUMPKIN-CHOCOLATE CHIP COOKIES

1 cup margarine
1 cup sugar
1 teaspoon vanilla
1 teaspoon baking soda
1/2 teaspoon salt
1 cup pumpkin

1 cup brown sugar
1 egg
2 cups flour
1 teaspoon cinnamon
1 cup oatmeal
1 cup chocolate chips

Combine ingredients and bake at 350° for 15 minutes.

HALLOWEEN TREAT

Form cereal or popcorn ball into a ball. For a stem add a slice of candy orange slice. Use pieces of raisin for eyes and nose.

PUMPKIN CUP

Cut the top off a large orange in a zig-zag pattern. Remove the inside pulp and fill with fruit or even candy. Put a toothpick on the top to be used as the eating utensil. Scratch a face onto the orange and go over the "face" with a permanent marker so the features show up.

JACK-O-LANTERN LUNCH

Make a regular sandwich but have a jack-o-lantern face cut out of the top slice bread.

PUDDING JACK-O-LANTERN

Cut off about one-half inch from the stem end of each orange. Remove pulp from orange top and bottom. With a knife cut jack-o-lantern faces into each orange shell. Fill each jack-o-lantern with 1/2 cup pudding. Add a cinnamon stick into the top. Replace tops. Refrigerate.

PUMPKIN PUDDING

16 ounces pumpkin
4 cups milk
1 teaspoon pumpkin pie spice

6 ounces instant vanilla pudding
4 teaspoons vanilla

Combine and put into bowls or orange jack-o-lanterns. Serve with whipped cream on top.

TAFFY APPLES

8 apples
1 can sweetened condensed milk
1/2 cup sugar
1/2 cup corn syrup
1/3 cup packed brown sugar

Put in a pan and bring to a boil, stirring constantly, until temperature reaches 235°. Remove from heat; add 1 tablespoon butter, stir. Roll apples in taffy; then in chopped nuts, if desired. Place on waxed paper.

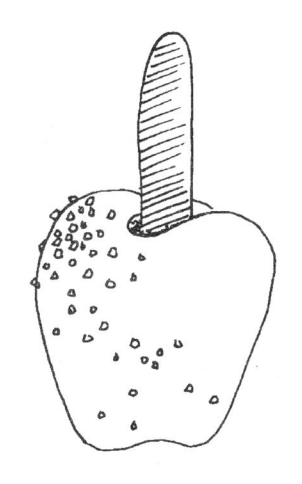

RAINBOW POPCORN BALLS

1 cup corn (unpopped)
1 cup sugar
1 cup white corn syrup
1-3 oz. package any flavor gelatin

Pop corn as usual. Mix sugar, syrup and gelatin in saucepan bringing to a boil. Stir until gelatin is dissolved. Pour over popped corn and make into balls.

HAYSTACKS

6 ounces semi-sweet chocolate pieces
1/2 cup chunky peanut butter
1-3 ounce can chow mein noodles

Melt chocolate and peanut butter on 50% power in the microwave. Stir after two minutes. Add noodles; toss well with fork. Drop clusters of haystacks onto waxed paper. Cool. Makes 3 dozen.

HALLOWEEN ICE CUBE

Add this "chilling" ice cube to punch. Buy a disposable latex glove at the drugstore. Fill the glove with water, seal it with a rubber band and freeze it. To give the glove a rounded shape, rest it over an item in the freezer. When you are ready to serve the punch, run warm water over the "hand" and the glove will slide off. Drop the "icy fingers" into the punch bowl.

CHOCOLATE SPIDERS

One 8-ounce chocolate bar
2 cups crisp rice cereal
1/2 cup shredded coconut

Melt chocolate bar one to two minutes in the microwave at 50% power. Stir in rice cereal and coconut. Drop from teaspoon onto waxed paper. Refrigerate until set. Makes 2 dozen.

PUMPKIN PARTY PUNCH

46 ounces apple juice or cider
1-30 ounce can pumpkin pie mix
1 quart vanilla ice cream
1 quart lemon-lime soda, chilled

Combine apple juice and pumpkin mix. Chill. Just before serving combine pumpkin mixture and ice cream in punch bowl; stir until smooth. Gently stir in soda. Yield: 4 1/4 quarts.

JACK-O-LANTERN JUMBLE

1/4 cup smooth peanut butter
1/4 teaspoon garlic powder
3/4 cup cocktail peanuts
2 1/4 teaspoon Worcestershire sauce

1 cup candy corn
8 cups crisp cereal
1/2 teaspoon salt

Preheat oven to 250°. Melt peanut butter with margarine in large shallow roasting pan in oven until shiny and soft (about 5 minutes). Remove and stir in salt, garlic powder and Worcestershire sauce until mixture is smooth. Add cereal and nuts; mix until all pieces are coated. Bake in oven for 1 hour, stirring every 15 minutes. Remove from oven and stir in candy corn. Spread on paper to cool.

SUPER SEEDS 'N STUFF

1 cup sunflower seeds
1 cup pumpkin seeds
1/2 cup sesame seeds
1 cup ready-to-eat cereal
1 cup raisins
1 cup dried fruit (chopped)
1 small package chocolate chips
1 cup almonds or walnuts or both

Put all in a large bowl to mix well. Eat by the handfuls.

JACK-O-LANTERN CAKE

Bake your favorite cake in an ovenproof bowl. Cool in bowl for 10 minutes and then remove. Cool on racks. Slice rounded tops from cake. Cut a 2 1/2-inch piece from a large banana to use for a stem. Frost the cake with orange icing; frost the stem green. Cut two eyes, a nose and a mouth from a red fruit roll, press into the icing of the cake.

PUMPKIN SEEDS

Keep the seeds when you clean out your pumpkin for your jack-o-lantern. Melt 3 or 4 tablespoons of butter in a pan, add a dash of Worcestershire sauce. Mix together with seeds. Spread on a cookie sheet and sprinkle with a little salt. Bake at 350° until the seeds are brown and crisp. Stir occasionally.

WITCHES BLUEBERRY PANCAKES

1 1/4 cups flour
2 1/2 teaspoons baking powder
3 Tablespoons granulated sugar
3/4 teaspoon salt
1 egg, beaten
3 Tablespoons melted oil
1/2 cup washed blueberries

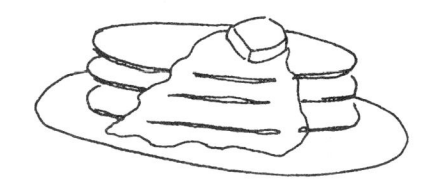

Combine ingredients and bake on hot griddle pan.

WITCHES DRINK

2 cups apple juice
1/2 cup orange juice
1/4 teaspoon cinnamon
2 to 3 cloves

Simmer on the stove for 20 to 30 minutes. Makes 5 servings.

HONEY JACKS

1/2 cup (6 Tablespoons) honey
1/4 cup butter or margarine
6 cups popped corn
1 cup shelled peanuts

Heat honey and butter in a saucepan until blended. Cool. Pour over popcorn mixture which has been mixed with peanuts, stirring as you pour. When well-coated, spread on a jelly roll pan in a single layer. Bake at 350° for 5 to 10 minutes or until crisp, stirring several times. The difference between crisp (no brown) and burnt can be a matter of minutes. Package in individual plastic bags.

THANKSGIVING

MAY GOD PLEASE ALWAYS GIVE US MORE PEOPLE TO LOVE THAN WILL FIT AROUND OUR DINING ROOM TABLE.

CRANBERRY SLUSH

2 cups chilled cranberry juice
1 Tablespoon lemon juice
2 scoops orange sherbet

Mix cranberry juice and lemon juice. Pour mixed juices into two glasses and top each with a scoop of sherbet.

SWEET POTATO BALL

Use marshmallow in center and put sweet potato around the marshmallow. Roll in crushed corn flakes. Bake for 10 minutes at 350°.

TURKEYS FROM APPLES

Use apples as the body. Use feathers cut from orange peels and attach with toothpicks to the apple. Cut the head and feet from heavy paper. Attach toothpicks to paper with tape and then insert into apple.

INDIAN DRIED APPLES

Core and peel apples. Slice through into circle shapes. Run a string through and hang the apples up in the sun until they are dry. Take them inside at night. Store them in airtight container in a cool place.

FERMENTY (Pudding like Pilgrims used to make.)

5 cups milk
1 Tablespoon butter
1/4 teaspoon nutmeg
2 Tablespoons raisins
   (soaked in water)

1/4 cup sugar
1/2 teaspoon cinnamon
3/4 cup cracked wheat
Sugar to top with

Heat milk with sugar, butter, spices. Add cracked wheat and soaked raisins. Let mixture simmer and stir often. When it thickens, remove from heat. Pour into serving dishes and sprinkle with sugar.

CREAM PUFF HORN OF PLENTY

Two packages frozen pastry sheets
Aluminum foil – four 18-inch squares

Using double sheets of aluminum foil, shape into a cornucopia. Hold edges together with paper clips.

Thaw the frozen pastry sheets for 30 to 40 minutes. On floured surface, roll out the pastry and cut dough into strips about 1 1/2 inches by 14 inches. Starting with point of cone, begin to wrap the dough strips around the foil. Wrap one strip around the tip of the cone. As it comes around brush 1/4 inch of the strip beneath with an egg glaze (one egg and two teaspoons of cold water, beaten together). Gently press the strip on top to adhere to other strip. Continue wrapping until cone is covered. Bake at 425° until golden brown. NOTE: Do not get egg glaze on aluminum foil or you will not be able to remove foil after baking. When cool, remove aluminum foil and cornucopia can be filled with your favorite recipe or cream puffs.

Serve sweet potatoes or cranberries in hollowed out orange half.

THANKSGIVING CRANBERRY CRUNCH

1 cup uncooked oats
1/2 cup flour
1 can whole cranberries
1 cup brown sugar
1/2 cup butter

Mix oats, flour and brown sugar together; cut in butter. Spoon half of the flour mixture into a greased 9 x 9-inch pan; cover with cranberries. Add remaining flour mix. Bake 45 minutes at 350°. Serve with ice cream, if desired.

TURKEY DINNER ROLLS

1 pound frozen bread dough
3 to 4 tablespoons all-purpose flour
Yolk of a large egg, beat with 1 teaspoon water
Accents as desired – sliced almonds, seeds, dried herbs, sprinkles, sugar, etc.
Small pretzel sticks

Place dough on floured surface, knead in additional flour so no longer sticky. Roll dough out to 1/4-inch thickness. Cut out turkey body parts. Place on a greased cookie sheet. Brush with egg glaze. While egg glaze is still wet, decorate turkey as desired. Let rise, uncovered, 5 to 10 minutes. Bake turkeys at 375° until golden brown.

EDIBLE TURKEY TREAT

Use melted chocolate chips for "glue". Make turkey with a chocolate star candy for "feet"; fudge-striped cookie for "feathers"; caramel for "body" and piece of candy corn for "beak".

EDIBLE CRANBERRY CANDLES

1 pound can whole cranberry sauce
1 cup boiling water
3 ounces strawberry gelatin
1 Tablespoon lemon juice
1/4 teaspoon salt
1/2 cup mayonnaise
1 apple, diced
1/4 cup chopped walnuts

Heat cranberry sauce, strain. Combine cranberry juice, water, gelatin, stirring until dissolved. Add lemon juice and salt. Chill until partially set. Add mayonnaise, beat until fluffy. Fold in cranberries, apples, walnuts. Stir. Chill until partially set. Fill cranberry sauce can 3/4 full for largest candle – spoon remaining mixture into assorted cans or glasses. Chill until firm. Unmold. Decorate as desired.

TURKEY CUP OF FRUIT

1/2 orange, 1/4 apple, 1/4 banana
Celery leaves, lettuce leaf, carrot round

Cut the orange in half, scoop out center. Dice the orange center and combine with other fruits. Fill the orange cup with diced fruit. Add a toothpick for the neck, a carrot round for the head and half a toothpick for a beak. Stick celery leaves in the back for feathers.

CHRISTMAS PUNCH

Two 6-ounce cans pink lemonade concentrate, thawed
1 pint vanilla ice cream, softened
1 quart milk
1 teaspoon green food coloring
1 pint vanilla ice cream (hard)

Mix lemonade concentrate and soft ice cream in a punch bowl and beat until smooth. Blend in milk; tint with food coloring, chill. Top with scoops of vanilla ice cream. Makes about 14 servings.

COOKIE WREATH

Serve various cookies on a large platter and put them in the shape of a wreath. Add a bow at the bottom of cookie wreath.

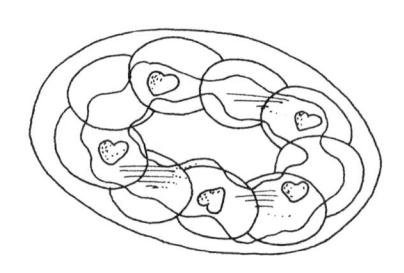

CHRISTMAS CHEER

Serve cranberry juice topped with lime sherbet.

SANTA COOKIES

Use peanut-shaped cookies. Add white icing on the bottom for his beard. On top put white icing for the hat. Add red sprinkles on the top part of the hat and attach a miniature marshmallow on the side of the hat. Add chocolate chip eyes and red hot for nose.

HOLIDAY DRINK

Hang a candy cane over the edge of a cup or glass to make that holiday drink special.

MINI-WREATH SANDWICHES

5 ounce jar Cheddar cheese food spread
3 ounces cream cheese, softened
1 Tablespoon chopped onions
1/8 teaspoon garlic powder
10 slices white or wheat bread
1 cup fresh parsley, dill or watercress
Sliced pimento

In food processor or blender blend all spread ingredients until smooth. Using a two-inch cookie cutter cut rounds from bread slices. Spread rounds with spread. Press parsley around edges to form a wreath. Garnish with pimento. Refrigerate.

ALMOND PINECONE

1 1/4 cup whole natural almonds
8 ounce package cream cheese, softened
1/2 cup mayonnaise
5 crisply cooked bacon slices
1 Tablespoon chopped green onion
1/2 teaspoon dill weed
1/8 teaspoon pepper

Combine cream cheese and mayonnaise, mix well. Add crumbled bacon, onion, dill and pepper; mix well. Cover; chill overnight. Form cheese mixture into the shape of a pinecone on a serving platter. Beginning at narrow end, press almonds at a slight angle into cheese mixture in rows. Continue overlapping rows until all cheese is covered. Garnish with artificial pine sprigs. Serve with crackers.

CANDIED POINSETTIAS

Large candied cherries may be cut to resemble poinsettias. Cut the cherry lengthwise into petals. Arrange petals on bread to resemble the flower. Use citron for leaves and stems.

CANDY CANE BALLS

Soften vanilla ice cream so you can make nice rounded balls. Crush candy canes. Combine crushed candy canes with red and green cookie decorating sugar. Roll the frozen balls of vanilla ice cream in this sugar.

COOKIE ORNAMENT PARTY FAVORS

Use cookie cutters to cut cookie dough into various holiday shapes. Sprinkle with green-tinted sugar and decorate with red candies or as desired. Place a dry bean in the top center of each cookie prior to baking. After baking, remove the bean and insert a ribbon to create a tree ornament.

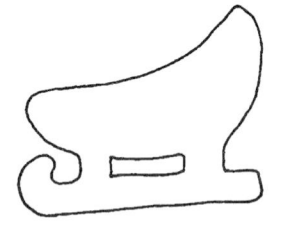

SNOW-TIPPED TREES

Spread green icing around a sugar ice cream cone. Turn the cone upside down and while icing is soft, add popped popcorn to the icing (about 1/2 cup of popcorn per cone). Add red cinnamon candies in between the popcorn to decorate the tree. Entire tree is edible.

DRUM CAKE

Bake two layers of your favorite cake. Frost with white fluffy frosting. To decorate press striped peppermint candy sticks at angles into icing all around the cake. Set a maraschino cherry at the ends of each stick. Cross 2 candy sticks on top of the cake for drum sticks.

GINGERBREAD HOUSE

This is an easy version that does not require much time. To one Gingerbread mix, add 1/3 cup water. Mix well and roll out into 1/2" thickness. It will work best if you take the time to make a cardboard pattern, but for a guideline, the base of the house will be about 4" x 6" and 3 1/2" high to the eave line. You will need sections as illustrated below:

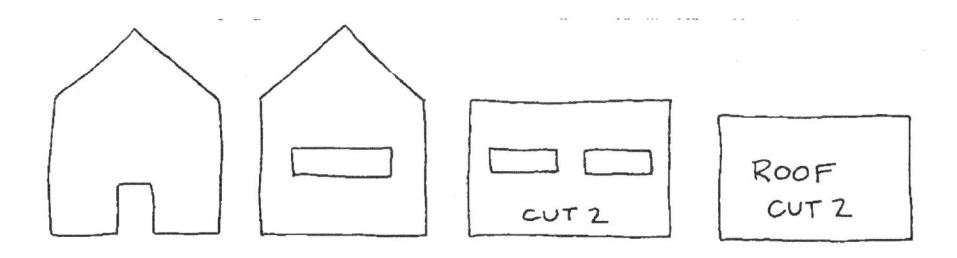

Design the door and windows before baking, but do not take the pieces out until after baking. Extra dough can be molded into little snowmen. Bake on a greased sheet without allowing the edges to get burnt (approximately 15 minutes). The house is "glued" together with frosting cement. Use toothpicks when or where necessary. Use the frosting cement to hold the base of the house to the plate so that it will stand. Dry the frame before adding roof.

GUMDROP POPCORN BALLS

4 cups miniature marshmallows
1/2 cup margarine
1/4 teaspoon salt
1/2 teaspoon vanilla
3 quarts popped corn
1 1/4 cups cut-up gumdrops

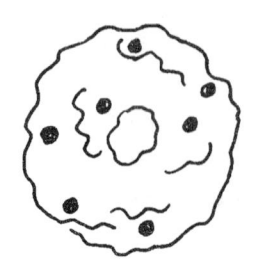

Melt margarine or butter, marshmallows and salt in a saucepan over low heat. Remove from heat and add vanilla. Mix. Mix popcorn and gumdrops in a separate bowl, then add marshmallow mixture. With clean hands, shape the mixture into balls. Put the balls on a greased cookie sheet until cool.

RELISH YULE TREE

Cover styrofoam cone with lettuce or parsley by attaching with toothpicks. Place styrofoam tree in the center of a serving tray. Arrange broccoli and cherry tomatoes with toothpicks as "ornaments" for the tree. Circle the base of tree with cauliflower.

CANDY CANE ICING

1 pound powdered sugar
1/2 cup softened butter
2 T. milk
1 1/2 teaspoons peppermint extract
4 medium-sized candy canes

In a large bowl mix all ingredients except candy canes. Put candy canes into a paper bag and hit with a hammer to crush into small pieces. Add some into the icing and save some of the crushed candy to add on top.

SNOWBALL CHEESE BALL

Two 8-ounce packages cream cheese
1/3 cup minced pineapple, well drained
1/3 cup bell pepper, minced
1/3 cup pecans, minced
1 cup coconut, shredded

Mix everything except coconut using your hands. Divide cheese mixture into two balls and roll into coconut pressing it into the cheese as you shape it.

CANDY SLEIGHS

1 chocolate candy bar
2 candy canes, miniature
2 gummy bears

"Glue" candy canes onto the side of the chocolate candy bar to create a sleigh. "Glue" gummy bears sitting on the top of candy bar. "Glue" can be melted chocolate morsels. Add a string of red licorice for rope, if desired.

CHRISTMAS TREE CAKE

On layer cake make the shape of a Christmas tree with green-tinted coconut. Make the base of tree with shaved chocolate. Roll red gumdrops on granulated sugar until flat. Cut out a star for the top. Insert candles in gumdrop stars and place on branches of tree. Add silver bead candy for trim.

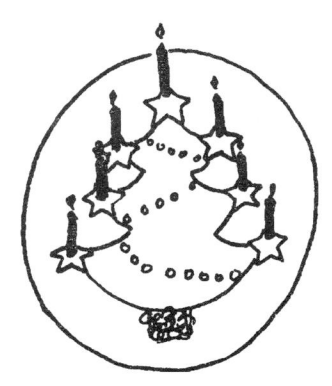

REINDEER SANDWICH

1 peanut butter and jelly sandwich
1 maraschino cherry
2 raisins
2 pretzel sticks

Cut prepared sandwich into a triangle. Place cherry on bottom for nose. Use raisins for the eyes and the pretzel sticks for antlers sticking them out of the top.

CHICKEN POINSETTIAS

2 cups diced cooked chicken
1/2 cup celery, chopped
2 pimentos, diced
1/2 cup mayonnaise
1/2 teaspoon dry mustard
1/2 teaspoon salt
1/4 teaspoon red pepper sauce
4 large tomatoes
Salad greens
2 sprigs fresh dill, snipped

Combine chicken, celery, pimentos. Blend salad dressing, mustard, salt and red pepper sauce. Toss 2/3 of the dressing mix with chicken mix. Chill. Reserve remaining dressing. Cut tomatoes in sixths, almost through to the bottom. Spread open slightly to form flowers. Fill centers with chicken salad; place on salad greens. Serve with remaining dressing. Garnish with dill.

HOT CIDER

1 gallon apple cider   1/2 gallon cranberry juice

Heat with four cinnamon sticks.

TOBOGGAN TREATS

Loosely roll up one end of striped-colored sticks of gum for the front of toboggan. (If gum cracks, hold between fingers to warm up and make more pliable). "Blue" bear-shaped graham cookies to toboggans with dots of icing. Decorate bears with icing, if desired.

VEGETABLE WREATH

Staple parsley to a styrofoam wreath form, overlapping to completely cover the form. Place the wreath in the center of a large serving tray. Toothpick vegetables (carrot curls, radish roses, broccoli and cauliflower florettes, whole mushrooms, celery) to the wreath. Insert a dish of your favorite dip in the center of the wreath.

CHOCOLATE CHIP COOKIE WREATH

Make your favorite chocolate chip cookie recipe. Spread one-half of dough in a 12-inch pizza pan lined with foil. Invert a four-inch oven proof bowl or custard cup in center. Grease the outside of bowl. Carefully remove from the two pans after cool. Decorate as desired. Makes 2 wreaths.

SNOWFLAKES

1 1/2 cups shredded toasted coconut
20 large marshmallows
1/4 cup evaporated milk

To toast coconut, spread coconut in a shallow pan. Place in a preheated 350° oven until lightly browned. Stir frequently. Cook 8 marshmallows and 1/4 cup evaporated milk in top of a double boiler, stirring constantly. When marshmallows dissolve, remove from heat but leave mixture over hot water. Cut 12 marshmallows in half. Dip marshmallows one at a time into mixture. Drop on waxed paper after rolling in shredded coconut.

BUTTER PECAN FUDGE

3 tablespoons butter
3 tablespoons milk
1 package butter pecan frosting mix

Melt butter in milk in double boiler. Add frosting and stir until smooth. Heat for 5 minutes, stirring occasionally. Pour into a greased 8-inch pan and let stand until firm.

HAPPY ELF CAKE

3 cups flour
1 teaspoon salt
2 cups sugar
1 teaspoon soda
6 tablespoons cocoa

2 teaspoons vanilla
2 teaspoons vinegar
10 Tablespoons salad oil
2 cups cold water

Combine dry ingredients and pour into a 9 x 9-inch pan. Make the elf's face by poking two "eyes" (holes) and a large smiling mouth into dry mixture. In one "eye" pour the vanilla, in the other, vinegar. In "mouth" pour the oil.

"Wash the face" by pouring cold water over all. Stir well, bake in preheated 375° oven for 30 to 35 minutes.

HOLIDAY CRAFTS

HOMEMADE VALENTINES

Cut a heart shape out of red construction paper. Attach a stick of chewing gum and add the words, **"Valentine, I'm stuck on you!"**

Make your own **valentine message** and attach to a popsicle stick.

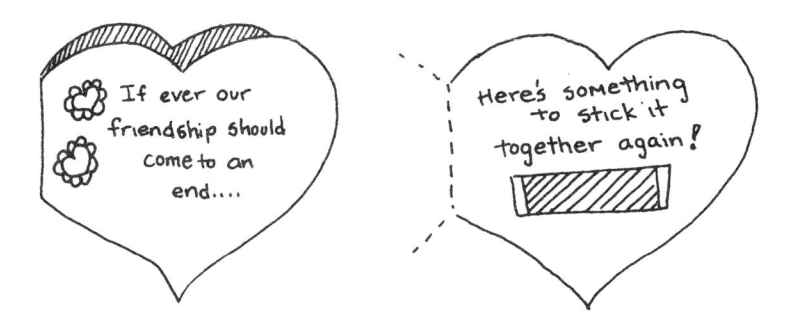

Cut out a **heart-shaped greeting card** out of red construction paper. On the outside write, "If ever our friendship should come to an end . . ." Then when you open the card up, the inside greeting should say, "Here's something to stick it together again!" Attach a stick of chewing gum to the card.

Help your child make a **valentine mailbox**. Take a shoebox and cut an opening on the top to insert the cards. Decorate the box and the greetings can be enjoyed over and over.

Make **valentines** by cutting out hearts in a chain like paper dolls.

Make **"fruity" valentines** by cutting an apple or potato into the shape of a heart. Dry it thoroughly. Press cut side of fruit on a red ink pad. Press onto brightly colored paper.

Take thick white paper and cut into the shape of a **bookmark**. Cut different shapes of hearts and arrows and paste onto the bookmark and trim the border with ribbon or lace.

Recycle your old valentine cards. Cut out the hearts, cupids, etc. and paste onto thick white paper and fold into a card of your own. Write your personal message.

Make a **heart puzzle** so that the person then has to put the puzzle together to read the message.

Reminisce into the 1800's when the **hand-in-heart design** for love tokens was popular. Trace the child's hand onto a piece of heavy paper. Add ribbon and lace for a cuff, add a heart cut from red paper or a doily and attach into the palm of the hand. The heart can be decorated with glitter, beads, paint and lace. On the reverse side of the hand you can add your personal valentine message. The traditional inscription reads, "Hand and heart shall never part. When this you see, remember me!"

Children love **valentine jigglers**. Have the child trace their hands onto green construction paper. Draw a red heart for the face, purple eyes, green nose, purple mouth, purple accordion pleated legs and purple according pleated arms.

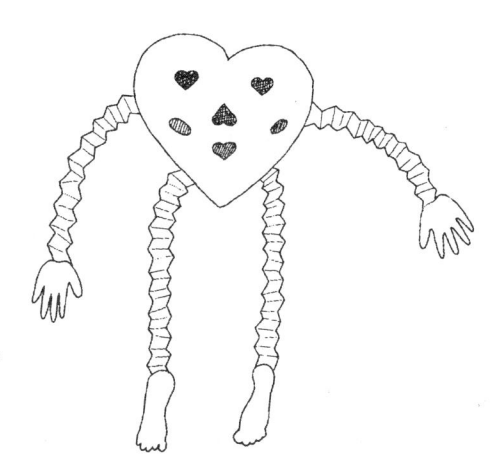

Hang **"Kissing Valentine Magnets"** onto your refrigerator during February.

       Fish 1:   White felt heart trimmed with pink heart for lips and red hearts for fin and tail.

       Fish 2:   Red felt heart trimmed with pink heart for lips and white hearts for fin and tail.

Add magnetic strips on the back of both fish after adding eyes to each fish.

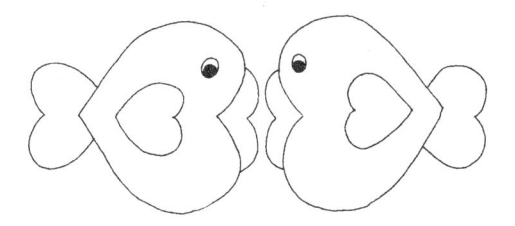

Consider a **valentine piñata** for your Valentine Party. Decorate with stickers, doilies, and old cards.

Have children make **valentine placemats** instead of cards. Cut sturdy posterboard into placemat size. Have child add a collage of photos, drawings, stickers, etc. When the paper is decorated and signed, cover with clear laminating paper and bind edges with colored plastic tape.

EASTER FUN

An **Easter egg hunt** – indoors or out – is always great fun. My children enjoyed finding the baskets as much as what was inside the basket. Add some hidden peanuts in the shell to provide extra hunting fun. Consider a moonlight egg hunt for older children.

Stenciling your colored eggs makes a nice designed egg. Purchase or make your own stencil pattern.

You can make your own **Easter egg dye**. Mix together 1/4 teaspoon food coloring, 3/4 cup boiling water and one tablespoon vinegar. Add one teaspoon vegetable oil to bowl of color for "marbled" look.

A small **bunny basket** makes a great classroom treat, party favor, or table decoration. Add pompons and felt to various sizes of mushroom baskets.

Make a **washcloth bunny** for the Easter baskets. Use one washcloth per bunny and roll up as the diagram indicates. Secure head with a rubber band and decorate face with felt pieces.

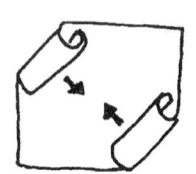

Easter egg animals are a fun change for the children. Hard boil and dye eggs as desired. When they are dry, use glue to attach the things listed below to the eggs. Use felt-tip markers to draw faces and decorate the bodies. You can make your own stands for the animals by using construction paper.

Pig: Use a pink-colored egg. Curl a pink pipe cleaner tightly for a snout and a more relaxed curl for the tail. Cut out pink paper ears. Use a marker to draw a face and decorate.

Lion: Start with a yellow-colored egg. Cut elongated triangles from orange tissue paper for the mane. Make a tail of braided yard, then tie it with a tissue paper bow. Cut out yellow paper ears and black paper whiskers.

Mouse: Use a blue-colored egg. Draw a face with a marker and add pink pompons for ears, pink paper whiskers and a pink pipe cleaner tail.

Bunny: Cut ears and paws from paper. Add a cotton ball tail and white whiskers.

Turtle: Use four mini pompons for the feet and a little curled pipe cleaner for the tail. Decorate another mini pompon with paper eyes and a mouth.

"There is only one success — to be able to spend your life in your own way."

Christopher Morley

Decorate a **drink cup** for the classroom parties. Cut out a bunny design from paper, decorate as desired and staple on to the drink cup. Fill with goodies.

Consider some **alternative decorating ideas.**

- paint designs with old nail polish
- scribble on eggs with crayons before putting in the dye.
- attach small candy pieces onto egg using cake decorating gel as the "glue"
- cover egg with stickers
- draw designs onto egg with cake decorating gel and then sprinkle with cookie decorating pieces
- put glue on egg and add glitter

Use **plastic eggs from panty hose**. Cut strips of tissue paper, multi-colored. Add a little water to glue. Dip the strips of tissue into glue mixture lightly and dab strips onto the egg form. Put in a festive basket to display.

Make an **Easter egg bunny nut cup** starting with an all-white margarine container. Decorate the front with a bunny face of purchased eyes and a pink pompon nose. Put white cotton balls on the side of the container and the back for cheeks and tail. Attach ears made from pink felt and a white pipe cleaner lining the felt for support.

Cut **Easter shapes** out of colored posterboard. Punch holes around the edges neatly. Put candy on the posterboard. Cover with heavy duty plastic wrap and then lace up with colored yarn.

Here's another use for egg shells. Start **seedlings in empty egg shells**. Punch a small drainage hole in the base of each shell half; add soil and seed. Rest the shell pots in an egg carton while seeds germinate. When it's time to transplant into the garden, crack the shells a bit and set them in the ground with the seedlings. The eggshells will decompose as the plants take root and start to grow.

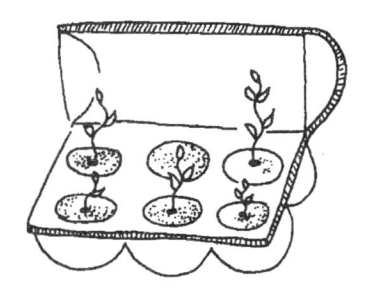

MOTHER'S DAY SURPRISES

Make a **corsage** for Mom to wear on her special day. Form a puffy pipe cleaner into a circular shape. Cut a circle out of colored posterboard to put the name on and then glue a corsage pin onto the back.

Use a paper doily for the base. Add a circle cut out of posterboard. Make three "flowers" – a piece of wrapped candy in the center of a piece of tissue paper. Add a bow and a **corsage** pin to the back.

FATHER'S DAY TREASURES

Make Dad a **terrarium**. Use a baby food jar. In the lid put green floral clay and stick grass to the clay. Add a miniature mushroom or animal. Put the jar over the lid so it looks like a terrarium.

Make your very own **ice cream for Dad**, without an ice cream maker. You will need: 1 cup milk, 1 cup heavy cream, 1/2 cup sugar, 1/2 teaspoon vanilla extract, crushed ice and rock salt. Put milk, heavy cream, sugar and vanilla in a one-pound coffee can. Close the lid tightly. Put the one-pound can into a five-pound coffee can. Pack in between the cans with ice and rock salt. Close the can tightly. Roll can back and forth with Dad on a hard floor for 10 minutes. Open outer can and throw out the rock salt and ice. Open inner can and stir ice cream, then reseal. Place small can back inside larger can and repack with ice and rock salt. Close can tightly and roll can back and forth another 10 minutes. Serve.

HALLOWEEN

What fun with **Halloween noise makers**. Use two heavy paper plates. Spray paint to color of choice. Decorate the front of one of the plates for face. Staple a large craft stick onto inside of one plate. Put beans inside the two plates. Glue plates together and trim. Use clothes pins to secure while drying.

For a **festive fall centerpiece**, hollow out a pumpkin and put a fall bouquet of flowers into it.

Decorate the porch of your home with a **spider web**. Start in the center and work your way out to make a spider web using heavy string. Make the desired size and attach a spider.

For a **Halloween door decoration** spray paint a rattan fan orange. When dry turn upside down and make a jack-o-lantern face on the front of the fan.

Make your own fast **clown make-up.** Add 1 to 2 drops of food coloring to 2 teaspoons of cold cream.

Create your own **Trick-or-Treat bags**. You will need a large brown grocery bag, an empty cereal box, strong yarn, glue, scissors, paper scraps, crayons and paint or markers.

Fold the top of the bag down inside the top about two inches. Cut the side strips from the cereal box. Place the box strips to the inside of the bag under the fold so it will not tear out. Use a hole puncher to punch two small holes through the box top on each side of the bag. String yarn handles through the bag and decorate.

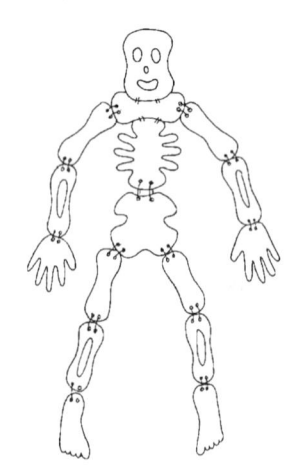

Make **hanging skeleton**. Cut the skeleton body parts out of paper plates. Punch holes to connect the adjoining part with paper clips so the parts will hang freely. Staple head and chest body parts together. Add a string so the skeleton can hang and move.

Lollipop covers make the holiday treat special. Cut double pieces of felt with pinking shears. Black for a cat, orange for a pumpkin. Hand sew the double pieces together or on a sewing machine leaving a space on the bottom to slip over a lollipop. Trim the pumpkin with green felt stem and black felt jack-o-lantern face. Trim cat with orange felt face pieces and pieces of fishing line for whiskers.

Numerous **Halloween costumes** can be made from a cardboard box, glue and odds and ends around the house. Turn your box into any number of costumes. Here are a few ideas to try:

GIFT BOX: Wrap the box with gift wrap. Decorate with ribbon and attach a large gift card. Have child wear curly ribbon in hair and on shoes to match.

DICE: Cut out holes in the box for head and arms. Cover the box with white paper and cut out and glue on dots made of construction paper or felt. Use red or black and wear matching leotards, gloves, hat or shoes as desired.

JACK-IN-THE-BOX: Decorate a box with brightly colored paper, yarn, buttons, glitter, ribbons, sequins. Have the child wear clown make-up. Staple accordion-folded construction paper around their neck. Add a silly hat. Make a lid from extra cardboard to be taped onto the box behind your child's head. A wind-up mechanism can be made from black pipe cleaners, with a styrofoam ball on the end. Use a spiral wire toy to cover each arm.

HOUSE: Spray paint or cover the box. Draw in a door and windows or cut them out. You can add shutters to windows. Decorate house as desired. Have child wear a "chimney" hat. Cover a smaller box with black paper and use bundles of cotton to resemble smoke coming out of the chimney.

COMPUTER: Cover the box with tin foil. Cut a slot at the top for "computer paper" by punching holes along sides of regular paper or paper towels. Add a logo and keyboard.

Design a **jack-o-lantern bag** by cutting two pieces of orange felt to the desired size. Sew on all edges except the top. Attach a ribbon and desired trimmings. Fill with candy.

Cover round lollipops with a white tissue. Tie with white yarn. Use a black marker to draw on a face. Give these **ghost lollipops** to trick-or-treaters.

Gourds make great **plant holders**. Dry gourd thoroughly before hollowing out. To prepare the gourd for carving, wipe off surface mold, soak in two quarts of water to which you have added 1/3 cup vinegar. Scrape off the softened outer layer of the ring, then hollow out as desired.

"You only live once – but if you work it right, once is enough."

Joe E. Lewis

THANKSGIVING

Cut a piece of brown netting six inches square. Fill with color **coated chocolate candy pieces**. Secure with a piece of thread leaving the end of the netting to resemble a tail. Shape half of a brown pipe cleaner into the shape of a turkey's head. Glue a small piece of red felt on the end for a beak. Glue eyes on each side of the head.

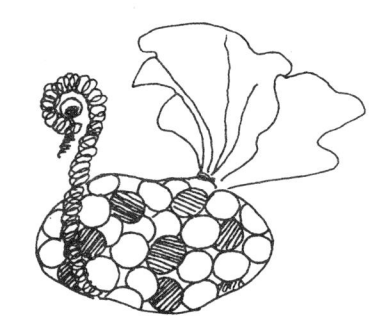

Trace your **child's hands** and decorate as desired to look like a turkey. Hang up for the holiday.

For Thanksgiving have children draw a picture of a **tree with branches** and no leaves on a piece of brown poster board. Cut it out and glue to a "sky" made of blue poster board. Take multi-colored construction paper and cut out leaf shapes. For each day in November have your child write an item they are thankful for on a leaf. Have the child attach the leaf to his tree. On Thanksgiving point out to the children that our life is like an empty tree until we take the time to count our blessings.

For your **turkey centerpiece** cut out the shape of a turkey head out of red felt. Add cotton inside for fullness after sewing together two pieces of red felt to form the head. Add black felt for the eyes on each side. Slip this fabric over the bottom of a fresh pineapple.

Make **Thanksgiving placemats** by cutting 12 strips 1-inch wide and 18-inches long from construction paper. Also, cut 18 strips that are 1-inch wide and 12-inches long in a different color. Weave strips in and out with the longest strip horizontal and the shorter strip vertical.

Have some **tepee fun** for Thanksgiving. You will need: eight 6-foot bamboo poles, two dropcloths, rope, masking tape, large felt-tipped marking pens.

Arrange the poles side by side on the ground and tie the ends together about one foot from the top. Stand the poles up with tied end up, then spread the poles apart. Push the end of the poles into the ground for stability. Drape dropcloths over the poles, leaving an opening for the door. Tape them randomly to the poles to keep the cloth in place. Decorate the tepee with the markers. Add a rug to cover the ground to complete your project.

Use miniature market baskets for the base of your **turkey nut cups**. Cut out various colored "feathers" from construction paper for the tail. Add a pipe cleaner head to the front of the basket. Attach eyes onto pipe cleaner. Fill with goodies.

CHRISTMAS

Make **cinnamon ornaments** with no baking! Mix 3/4 to 1 cup applesauce with one 4.12-ounce bottle of ground cinnamon to form a stiff dough. Roll out to 1/4-inch thickness. Cut with cookie cutters. Make a hole for the ribbon to hang. Carefully put on a rack to dry. Let air dry several days, turning occasionally. Makes 12 sweet smelling ornaments.

To make **pickling spice wreaths** spread white glue on the front of a wooden curtain ring. Press glued portion into a bowl of pickling spice. Add trims of ribbon, bells or miniatures. Add string to hang on the tree.

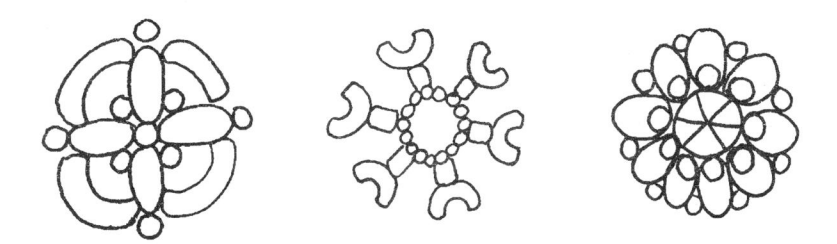

Use your imagination to create many shapes and designs from assorted **macaroni** pieces. Assemble these **ornaments** on waxed paper which can be easily removed after the ornaments are dry. Pour a small amount of glue onto the waxed paper, dip the edges of macaroni into the glue, form your own design. Tweezers can be used to handle the macaroni pieces easily.

Trace 1 foot and 2 hands of your child onto paper. Put the foot in front and the two hands in the back with thumbs out to make it look like a **reindeer**. Draw onto brown paper. Can decorate the face with circle eyes, red circle nose, draw on lips, eyelashes. How great to remember the size of those small hands and feet for later years.

Customize a **light switch cover** for the holidays. Cut Santa pieces out of red and white felt. Attach a copy of the following poem onto the beard.

**My eyes, how they twinkle,
My beard's white and rich,
My cheeks are so ruddy,
My nose a light switch!**

**Apply sticky tape
On the back of my face;
Then find a light switch
And push me in place.**

**Now just flick my nose
Your light will burn bright;
Flick again, all is dark.
MERRY CHRISTMAS!
Good Night.**

Make a **gumdrop tree** with a styrofoam tree for the base. Attach gumdrops with toothpicks. Add a piece of colored paper around the cone before attaching gumdrops, if desired, and then you do not have to completely cover the tree with gumdrops.

Cover a cardboard rectangle with red cotton corduroy and add holiday motifs cut from glitter-sprinkled cotton batting. The motifs will cling to the fabric without glue. For quick edging pin on a rope of cotton batting entwined with red and green string. Your **holiday banner** is ready to hang on the wall with velveteen ribbon.

For a **holiday mobile** attach ornaments to a straw wreath. Hang from a light fixture in the center of a room or in a hallway foyer.

Attach a magnetic strip to small Christmas ornaments and you have instant decorative **refrigerator magnets**.

An **ice cream cone ornament** can easily be made by gluing a bright colored glass Christmas ball onto any type of real ice cream cone.

Any holiday hard candy makes great **candy ornaments** as long as they have a pretty center. Lay the candy on a greased cookie sheet leaving room for the candy to spread. Bake in a preheated 300° oven for 10 minutes. Let cool two minutes. Make a hole at the top with a toothpick for hanging.

A simple **candy cane vase** is a pleasant holiday accent. Simply glue candy canes onto a plastic container or empty coffee can. Have the tops of the candy canes at the top. Seal the project with varnish and tie a bow around the candy canes.

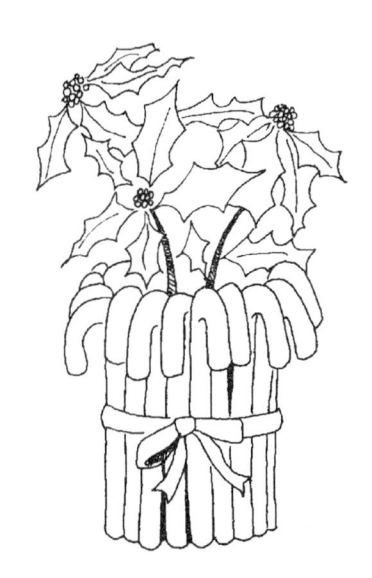

Make great decorating craft items with cotton crochet thread. Soak thread in full-strength liquid starch and wrap around an inflated balloon in a criss-cross fashion. When thread is dry, deflate the balloon and remove it from the top opening. If using as a basket, cut to desired size and then trim accordingly. If making a small size you can use as an ornament. Add trim to the **lacy-looking globe** as desired.

Create festive **decoupage bowls** out of cardboard plant liners. Use old Christmas cards with pretty scenes. If card is on thick paper, dip the card into hot water and peel off some of the paper backing so it will be easier to work with. Glue onto bowl. Then decoupage over the cards. Fill with candy, holly or pine cones.

Make an unusual **door decoration** by rolling down the top of a brown grocery bag and spraying it with green paint. Fill the bag with brightly colored wrapped boxes, greenery, candy canes. The paint protects the bag from the weather for outdoor hanging.

Help your child make a **personalized potholder**. Trace the child's hand onto a plain potholder. Embroider around the handprint or let the child paint it. Add the child's name and age.

To make a **waterproof** inexpensive **wreath** start with a coat hanger and bend it into a circle. Remove the hook. Using two 13-gallon large white kitchen garbage bags, cut each bag into approximately 200 strips, 6 inches long by 1 1/4 inches wide. Tie the strips onto the hanger one at a time. (This will keep the youngsters busy for a long time!) Continue with the entire amount pushing together to make the wreath full. Wire sprigs of holly or greenery onto the wreath, add a bow or decorate using your own imagination.

To make a **candy cane candle**, glue candy canes together with a red candle in the center. Glue with the tops of the candy canes at the bottom so it will stand up. Varnish and secure with a bow.

Add a **holiday scent** to your room with sweet smelling pine cones. Put glue on the edges of pine cones and sprinkle with ground spices (cinnamon, allspice, nutmeg and cloves). Place pine cones in a basket.

Make a **large lawn greeting** or perhaps a smaller size for a table top. The basic idea is the same. Paint boards with your desired festive theme and then attach together with hinges. Makes a great background for holiday photographs.

Make your very own **nut wreath centerpiece**. Cut out a piece of plywood into a circle shape of desired size. Cut out a hole in the center. Glue the inner and outer circles with pine cone petals. Cover the bottom of plywood with English walnuts. Let dry overnight. Glue various mixed nuts to form a wreath. Let dry overnight. Bake at 200° for 3 hours. When cool, spray with shellac to finish.

Kids love to make their own **Christmas decorations**. Anything can be magically transformed. Here are a few ideas:

Decorate any oatmeal box into **drummer boys' drum**. Fill.

Decorate **styrofoam balls** with assorted pipe cleaners, glitter, ribbon.

Decorate bright colored **wooden beads**.

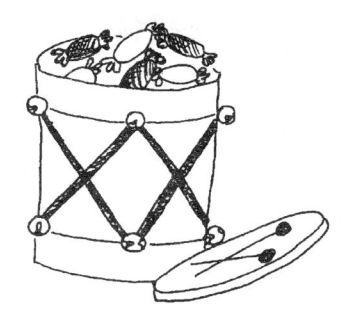

Make a **tin ornament** out of throw-away aluminum pie tins.

Turn last year's holiday cards into **placecards** for the table.

Make a **snowball tree** with a styrofoam cone. Add cotton balls by gluing on and then decorate with glitter.

Cut out your own **snowflakes** from plain or colored paper.

Add glitter, sequins, string to **pine cones**.

Put glue on the edges of **pine cones** and sprinkle with ground spices (cinnamon, allspice, nutmeg and cloves). Place scented pine cones in a basket.

Decorate an empty, clean orange juice concentrate can into a **pencil holder**. Attach a photograph to make special.

Make a **paper chain countdown** until Christmas. Add messages for each chain.

Make a **macaroni wreath** with macaroni glued onto a piece of paper into the shape of a wreath.

MAKE YOUR OWN FORTUNE COOKIES

Children love to help on this project – if not convenient, just have the children write the fortunes.

1/4 cup flour
1 tablespoon corn starch
2 tablespoons cooking oil
1/4 teaspoon vanilla
8 to 10 paper "fortune" cookie strips, either typed or written on pieces of paper or cut from magazines

2 tablespoons brown sugar
Dash of salt
1 egg white, beaten until stiff
3 tablespoons water

Combine flour, sugar, cornstarch and salt. Stir in oil and fold in egg white until mixture is smooth. Add flavoring and water and mix well. In a small skillet, an electric pan on medium heat or on a lightly greased griddle, pour one tablespoon of batter, spreading it to a 3-inch circle. Cook for 4 minutes or until lightly browned, turn with a spatula and cook for one more minute or until lightly browned, turn with a spatula and cook for one more minute. Batter will turn from beige to brown. Remove from griddle and quickly place "fortune" paper in the center of the circle. Fold in half over the edge of a glass, and then in half again. Hold for a few seconds until cool, then place in an empty egg carton to help cookie keep its shape. These get better with practice. This recipe make 8 to 10 fortune cookies. If they do not seem crisp enough for you, toast them in the oven at 300° for 10 minutes.

HOLIDAY HOME FRAGRANCE

4 cups water
1 stick cinnamon

1 teaspoon whole cloves
4 to 5 drops cinnamon or clove oil

Simmer all ingredients in an open pan on the stove. As fragrance diminishes, add more oil.

KEEP 'EM BUSY

> "Raising children is not for the faint of heart."
>
> **Roz Chast**

PAINTED SNOWBALLS – To brighten up a winter's day, make snow paint. Make several pitchers of colored water with a half dozen drops of food coloring per container. The bolder the colors, the better. Let the kids color the snow and make colored snowballs with squirt guns or spray bottles. The dye will harmlessly melt away.

FLYING SAUCERS – Tape two paper plates together to create a curved top and bottom. Glue a paper bowl to the center top to make a cabin for the crew. Let dry. Use markers or crayons to draw insignias, windows, doors, etc. Designate a landing pad, then toss flying saucers through the air. See whose lands the closest to the pad.

BACKYARD BIRDWATCHING – Freeze melon seeds in empty egg cartons during the summer. When the thermometer drops, take cakes out of the freezer and use when needed.

PLANET MOBILE – Earth is in the solar system – planets move around the sun. Make your own solar system by drawing planets, stars and a sun on paper. Color, cut and glue each one to a piece of yarn. Tie the yarn to a hanger and presto – your own solar system.

CALENDARS – Have children draw their own picture for each month. Make a standard page with five rows of seven days in each row. Then fill in the numbers for each month. Get pages spiral bound together or use two or three small o-rings to keep together and punch holes to hang.

SOAP PAINT – 1 cup powdered detergent
4 teaspoons liquid starch
1 teaspoon powdered tempera paint

Beat detergent and starch with beater until peaks form. Add tempera and mix well. Paint away!

HOMEMADE PUTTY – Mix well: 2 parts white glue
1 part liquid starch

It needs to dry a bit before it is "workable". The putty may need a touch more glue or starch. You will have to experiment. It may not work well on a humid day. Store in an airtight container.

SIMPLE STILTS – You will need two tuna cans and two lengths of clothesline, each about four feet long. Wash cans and dry. Turn cans over and punch hole in either side. Thread clothesline through holes in cans and tie ends together. Cord may be wrapped with masking tape to prevent wearing against can.

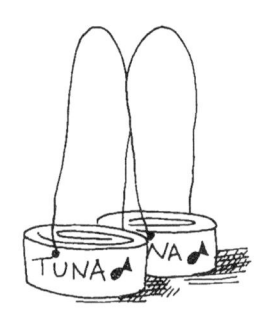

TISSUE PAPER FLOWERS – Cut out six pieces of tissue paper in two or more colors. Staple together in the center. Pull each layer up one-at-a-time and squeeze to look like a flower.

MILK CARTON HAIR – Cut a milk carton to about four inches high. Cover with self-adhesive paper. Have your child paint a face on one side. Fill with soil, sow some grass seed on top, water and watch the grass grow like hair.

BUBBLES – 1 cup lemon dishwashing liquid
1 teaspoon glycerin (available at drugstore)
1 cup white corn syrup
5 cups water

Mix all ingredients well. Works better if sits overnight.

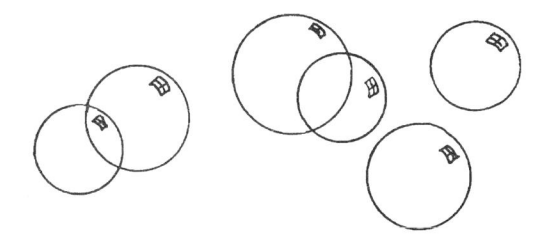

PLAY DOUGH – 1 cup white flour, 1/4 cup salt, 2 tablespoons cream of tartar. Mix in a medium pot. Combine and add 1 cup water, 2 teaspoons vegetable food coloring and 1 tablespoon oil. Cook over medium heat and stir about 3 to 5 minutes. When it forms a ball in the center of the pot, turn out and knead on lightly floured surface. Store in an airtight container.

CHILDREN'S WREATH – Have children decorate their own personal wreath. Simple straw forms are very inexpensive. Have a child decorate any way they choose – small toys or dolls, wrapped candy, bubblegum. Let the child hang on the door of his room.

HULA HOOP FOUNTAIN –   1 hula hoop
1 PVC fitting and washer
1 garden hose
1 hammer
1 nail
1 sharp knife

Punch holes two inches apart. Cut through the hula hoop and attach PVC fitting into the cut openings. Attach a garden hose and turn on for water fun!

GROWING SPROUTS – Sprouts are fun for children to grow because they grow so quickly. They can be grown in glass jars or small plastic bags. If you use glass jars, cover with a square of cheese cloth or nylon stocking and secure with a rubber band. If you choose small bags, stick 10 holes in the bottom of the bag with a large needle. Have children fill jar or bag with 1/8 to 1/4 full of sprout seeds. Fill the jar with warm water or zip up the bag and place it in a bowl of warm water. Soak seeds overnight. Have children drain the seeds well and place in a light place, but not in the direct sunlight. For the next 3 or 4 days, have the children rinse and drain the seeds daily. Place sprouts in the direct sunlight on the last day and they will green up more. Store sprouts in the refrigerator. Use on salads or sandwiches.

PAPER NECKLACE – Cut three triangles the same size. Fold paper end over a long string and glue. Roll paper tight. Wrap around the string and glue at the point. Repeat three times and tie string at the ends around your neck.

Put rubber bands on small children's drinking cups so they can more easily hold on to them.

DECOUPAGE BASKETS – Decorate baskets for any occasion simply by cutting out designs from fabric and then decoupage onto a basket. Spray paint basket first for color changes.

OVERNIGHT DRYING CLAY – Mix 1 cup cornstarch, 2 cups baking soda (1 lb.) and 1 1/4 cups cold water. Stir in a saucepan over medium heat for about 4 minutes until the mixture thickens to moist mashed potato consistency. Remove from heat, turn out onto a plate and cover with a damp cloth until cool. Knead as you would dough. Shape as desired or store in an airtight container or plastic bag. For color, add a few drops of food coloring to the water before it is mixed with starch and soda. Objects may be left to dry and then painted with water colors or acrylics. Dip in shellac or brush with clear nail polish for a sealer.

FLOWER BOUQUET – Make a floral clay into a ball shape and flatten on the bottom so it will sit flat when it dries. Stick dried flowers into clay. Cover the ball with a piece of gingham or other colorful fabric. Use pinking shears to cut top of fabric. Tie a ribbon around the center and you have your floral bouquet.

LIBRARY PASTE – Add 1 cup flour, 1 cup sugar, 1 teaspoon alum and 4 cups of water. Cook until becomes clear and thick. Add 30 drops oil of wintergreen or cloves and store covered.

BULLETIN BOARD – Purchase ceiling tile from local lumber yard. Cut to desired size and cover the edges with colored plastic tape.

WATER COLOR STREAMERS – You will need a glass jar, water, food coloring and a flashlight. Fill the jar with water. Add a drop of food coloring to the water and observe the color swirl as it travels down through the water. Try a different color. Shine the flashlight through the jar for water magic.

MAKING STENCILS – Fold a piece of construction paper in half. Draw a shape using the fold for your inside edge and cut along the drawn line. Open the paper and find your stencil.

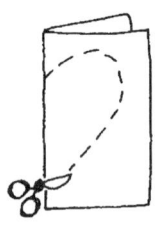

PERSONAL NOTE PADS – Find the small note pads so you know what size you will use. Cut felt to make a little book with note pad inside. Cut felt with pinking shears for a finished look. On the front put a picture of the child or his pet.

SNOWING JAR – Find a jar that has a tight fitting lid. Paint the lid, if desired. Place a figurine in the lid of the jar with window caulk. Rub a drop of dish soap on the figurine; careful not to use too much or it will bubble. Fill the jar with water and put some moth FLAKES (not crystals) in the jar for the snow. The drop of dish soap will prevent the flakes from sticking to the object.

FASHION SOAP BARS – Slowly slice off the soap's brand name with a warm paring knife. Scrape the surface until smooth. Attach flowers, lace, pictures or other decorations with polymer medium or glue. Melt a bar of paraffin wax in the top of a double boiler. Brush melted paraffin over the top of the decorations on soap. When dry, scrape off dripped wax from the sides. You can use a polymer medium or water base finish/adhesive to coat the soap.

FINGER PAINTS – Soak one envelope unflavored gelatin in 1/4 cup water. Combine 1/2 cup cornstarch and 3 tablespoons sugar, then gradually add 2 cups water. Cook slowly over low heat, stirring constantly, about five minutes. Remove from heat and add gelatin mixture. Divide into containers and add a drop or two of liquid dish detergent. Then stir in food coloring.

WINTER TREAT FOR BIRDS – 5 1/2 cups oatmeal, 3 1/2 cups corn meal, 12 ounces peanut butter, 3 1/2 cups wheat meal and 1 pound lard. Cook 4 cups water with 2 cups oatmeal for 2 minutes. Remove from heat, stir in lard and peanut butter. When cool enough to handle, add the remaining oatmeal, corn meal and wheat meal one cup at a time. Knead together until mixture is right consistency to pack into containers. Extra mixture can be stored in freezer until needed. You may want to pack it in half grapefruit shells and hang it on a tree.

PAPER SNOWFLAKES – You will need white typing paper, white glue, heavy-duty thread, scissors. Cut paper in half lengthwise. Fold crosswise into 1/2-inch according pleats. Cut away a semi-circle on each side in the middle of the paper. Cut 24-inch piece of thread, double thread and tie around the center to secure pleats. Cut out various shapes of paper to make your design a snowflake. Run a line of glue along one outside pleat of paper. Place thread-ends on glue strip. Open the pleats and sandwich threads with the opposite outside pleat. Open and glue together other sides of pleating to finish the snowflake. Knot ends of thread and use as a tree hanger, if desired.

CINDER GARDEN – Mix 6 tablespoons water and 6 tablespoons bluing salt. Let set one hour. Pour mixture over cinders or brick. Add a drop of food coloring in spots. Put it where it will not get bumped. Children like to watch this grow.

WALLPAPER PROJECTS – Purchase discontinued wallpaper books for numbers of craft projects with children.

Pleat the wallpaper to make a **fan**.

Make a wallpaper **angel** and add coordinated ribbons.

Cut designs out of inexpensive wallpaper and glue around a room for a **border**.

PAPER CHAINS – Cut strips of paper one-inch wide and five-inches long. Glue the ends together to form a circle. Slip one strip through another and glue ends together.

SEAL YOUR PICTURE FRAME – After your child creates his masterpiece put it in a frame. To seal the frame take a brown grocery bag and cut to size of the back of the frame. Wet paper (just run under the sink and dab off the excess water). Glue down while wet and it will tighten as the paper dries.

LETTER HOLDER – Use clear plastic lids to make a letter holder. Cut one lid in half and attach to the other lid with tabs of self-adhesive paper which is also the trim to decorate.

LIGHTWEIGHT GLUE – Egg white makes a good adhesive to glue the paper of kites. It holds well and is almost weightless.

PAPER MACHÉ PASTE – Mix a handful of flour, add water until gooey. Then add a pinch of salt. This recipe can also be used as a quickie finger paint concoction by adding some food coloring and working it on heavy paper or cardboard.

CLEAN THE HATS – Clean the hats of your sports fans by placing them on the top rack of the dishwasher while washing dishes. Let air dry.

PAPER CUPS – You can make a variety of playthings with plain paper cups:
1. Bells – just decorate and add a ringer inside the cup with a string or yarn.
2. Mini-Drum – Cover the paper cup with paper held in place by elastic or rubber band.
3. Telephone – Connect two paper cups with a long string and you have an imaginary telephone system.
4. Spyglasses – Attach two paper cups together with tape, punch holes out for eyes and attach string to go around head.

PAPER BAGS – Grocery brown paper bags make good costumes. Help children cut out facial features and room for the arms.

Decorate brown bags and use in a child's room for a garbage bag.

A smaller brown bag makes an excellent hand puppet. Make the "head" on the base of the bag.

PAPER PLATES – Transform your paper plates into:
1. Easter hats decorated with flowers and ribbon.
2. A clock to help learn the time.
3. Mail holders when the bottoms of two plates are stapled together.

FIRE LOGS – For each five gallons of water, add two teaspoons of detergent (either liquid or granule). Roll newspaper in tight rolls over chrome rod, then slip off. Soak newspapers overnight and stack so they can dry.

PUDDING PAINT – Kids will love! Lay down a surface of waxed paper and globs of instant pudding for fingerpainting. Must supervise!

POP-UP CARDS – Begin by folding a piece of plain medium-weight paper in half. A good size for the paper would be about five inches by eight inches, but you can vary the dimensions. Decide on a design for the pop-up such as a snowman, fish, candle, angel or any other fairly symmetrical design. Cut your pop-up design out of paper, glue on features or mark with paint or markers and then fold the figure in half down the center line from top to bottom. Fold back the two side tabs and glue them onto the card. Let dry before closing the card.

ENLARGE PATTERNS – To enlarge patterns draw a grid of parallel lines vertically and horizontally (at right angles) on paper or thin cardboard, spacing the lines as indicated. Then copy pattern on your grid, one square at a time. Cut out or trace the enlarged pattern.

SPECIAL STRAWS – Make a cutout in a circle or special shape and then use a hole puncher to make a hole in the top and bottom of your design. Let your child decorate. Then weave the straw in the one hole and out the other. Can add names or special messages. Works well as a place card for a party.

BEACH WEAR – Glue fake gems on to your plain rubber flip-flop sandals. Add buttons and bows to a simple straw hat. Fabric paint an oversized t-shirt for your child's beach robe.

PAPER CUP FLOWER – Using a small paper cup start at the drinking end of the cup. Cut a straight line all the way to the bottom of the cup. Do this the whole way around the cup. Stand the cup on a flat surface and flatten the sides out. This makes the petals. Color the petals. Tape or glue the straw or pipe cleaner on to make the stem. Make a few more for a bouquet.

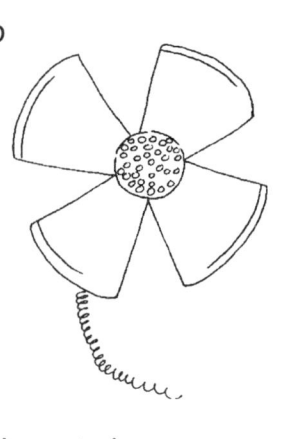

QUICK DOG BISCUITS – 1 jar strained baby food meat, 4 heaping teaspoons powdered dry milk, 6 heaping teaspoons wheat germ. Mix well. Roll into small balls and flatten on lightly greased cookie sheet. Bake at 350° for 10 minutes.

SALT PAINTING – Salt painting is an inexpensive art idea that can be used in the classroom or at home. Sand or salt are mixed with powdered tempera paint until salt is colored. Start with a small amount of white glue. Have child create a design on the paper with the glue. The child then sprinkles the colored salt onto the gluey areas to color in the design. Each child's design will be unique. Encourage the child to tell you a story about his design.

CLAY FOR PLAY – Mix 1 cup salt, 1/2 cup water and 2 tablespoons vegetable oil. Add 2 cups flour. After shaping, the clay can be baked at 250° for several hours. Good project for tree ornaments.

EGG CARTON JEWELRY – Let your imagination run wild as you create your own earrings, pins, pendants from egg cartons. Tear bits from the paper type egg cartons and glue the bits together forming a shape. Let dry completely. Paint, let dry. Glue on decorations, if desired. Spray with clear acrylic to seal. Attach back to earrings or pins.

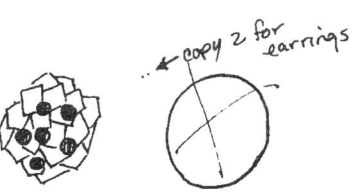

copy 2 for earrings

GET STAINS OUT – After all these projects your child will probably have stains in clothes. Add boiling water to 1/4 cup dishwasher detergent. Fill bucket up with water and soak overnight. Throw in washer.

HATS AND HORNS – Roll paper with the point at the top. Continue to roll with point at the top. Glue edge. Trim bottom and poke string through each side and tie. Trim point to make your horn.

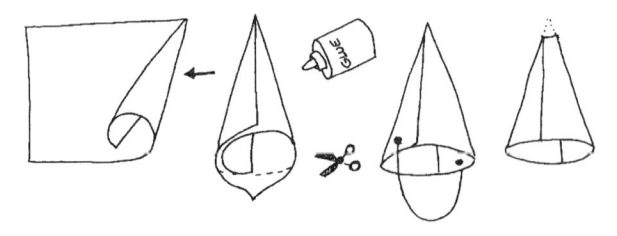

SMELL CARDS – You will need blotter paper, cotton swabs, plenty of different extracts such as vanilla, peppermint, almond, etc. Cut several squares from the blotter paper. Use the cotton swabs to spread the extract on one side of the blotter paper. When the squares are dry, they are ready to be smelled. Try using several kinds of extract on one card to create new smells.

BEAN BAGS – Sew three sides of two fabric squares together; add beans and sew up the fourth side. Perhaps use a small child's sock or mitten as a bean bag. Sew up the last side.

BALANCE FUN – Walk on a 4-inch by 4-inch piece of wood. Walk on an air mattress. Make tunnels out of cardboard boxes. Walk across a trampoline. Balance yourself on the curb.

> "Feeling gratitude isn't born in us – it's something we are taught, and in turn, we teach our children."
>
> **Joyce Brothers**

Mom, I'm Bored

Organize a household **scavenger hunt**.

Challenge your child to create their own **board game**.

Make a **stand** – sell traditional lemonade, flowers from your garden for Mother's Day, surplus vegetables, old toys, etc.

Make a **"house"** from large appliance boxes.

Have a **penny carnival** in your backyard – toss a ball into a basket; bowling game; beanbag toss. Use trinkets for prizes.

Make a homemade backyard **obstacle course**. Crawl under lawn chairs, through box tunnels, hop along a garden hose, dodge an oscillating sprinkler, balance a table tennis ball on a paper plate.

Hold **puppet shows** behind the sofa. Create puppets out of old socks, paper lunch bags, etc.

Cook in the fireplace.

Surprise someone with an **"unbirthday" party**.

Make your own **miniature golf course** using old doormats, carpet squares, placemats. Use long tables or pipes for fairways. Attach flags to sticks and play with wiffle balls.

Hold your own neighborhood **Olympics**. Pass out ribbons for winners.

Build **mud-brick architecture**. Mix water in soil until texture is like dough. Shape into rectangles and let set. Use a wet table knife to cut into various sizes. Make a new batch of mud for the mortar between layers.

Let child spend the day taking a roll of pictures on a **disposable camera**.

Let neighborhood children have a **"favorite vacation"** day. Children can bring mementos, dress to appropriate vacation, show video.

Plant a garden with your "helpers". Sunflowers are a hit with children because they virtually grow overnight.

Use your video recorder to make a **home movie**. Allow your child to invite friends for the cast.

Personalize your children's towels and washcloths with them one afternoon.

Make a **totem pole**. Cut the tops off 5 or 6 milk cartons. Make 2-inch slits in the corners, wedge the bottom of one inside the top of the carton beneath it. Cover with paper; decorate with photos.

Make **leaf prints**. Brush acrylic paint on the underside of a leaf. Place the painted leaf on a card or paper; cover with a paper towel. Roll a rolling pin over the paper. Remove towel; lift leaf carefully.

Build numerous **tents** in your house with old bed sheets.

Fasten a tiny flashlight to a large plastic kite for **night flying**.

Make a **punching bag**, stuff old rags into a duffle bag or pillows all lined up.

Plant a garden in an old children's wading pool.

Play a game by using **foreign-language flash cards** and gummed labels. Attach flash cards of foreign words to household objects.

FIELD TRIP ADVENTURES

Get permission from a **local bank** or store to have children paint their windows for the approaching holiday.

Let each child spend $5 at a **thrift shop** – how fun to see what they choose – dress-up clothes, old valuables, etc.

"Pick your own" vegetable or berry farm.

Take **walks with** different things in mind –

>Garden Walk
>Windy Day Walk
>After-a-Rain Walk
>Fall Leaves Walk
>Good Health Walk

Community Services – telephone company, post office.

Coordinate field trips with the meaning of words and how to do **everyday errands**.

Factories where common goods are made – children especially like candy and snack items.

Fish hatchery

Dairy farm

Public auction

Fire and police departments

Newspaper office

Water treatment plant

Recycling center

Local radio or television station

Brewery or soft drink company

Bird watching

Sleep in a cave

Visit a college

Spend the night at the local zoo in tents

Gas station – pump gas

Camping

Courthouse

Hardware store – find nails, screwdriver, etc.

Fast food restaurant

Supermarket – locate cereal, bread, etc.

Pet show

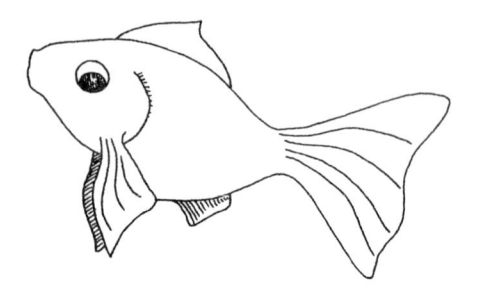

MOM, LET'S PLAY

Kids will love the same **games** you loved as a kid. If you've forgotten the rules, check your local library. Remember these?

- Red Light, Green Light
- Leapfrog
- Red Rover, Red Rover
- Stick Ball
- Dodge Ball
- Hide and Seek
- Punch Ball
- Duck, Duck, Goose
- Statue
- Simon Says
- Jacks
- Monkey in the Middle
- Capture the Flag
- Freeze Tag
- Kick the Can
- Blind Man's Bluff
- Hopscotch
- Mother, May I?
- Jump Rope
- Cat's Cradle

SHOE RACE – Everyone removes their shoes and places them in a pile. Then on signal they race to find their own and put them back on. The age of the children will determine whether they have to tie or buckle the shoes.

VASELINE RELAY – Put vaseline on all noses. Have cotton balls on a cookie sheet on the other side of the room. Divide the group into teams. Each child has to put their nose down to have a cotton ball stick. The team that has the most to stay on their noses wins.

SCRAPBOOK ABC'S – Make an alphabet picture scrapbook using old greeting cards to teach children their ABC's. For example, "A" is for angel (use a card showing an angel); "B" is for baby, etc.

STACKED DECK – Turn a deck of cards into a stack of interlocking building blocks and the sky's the limit. With each card, use scissors to make one-inch snip in the middle of all four edges. Then, join together cards by interlocking the notches to building towers, tunnels and bridges.

TELL ME A PICTURE – One player looks at a simple picture or photograph without letting the other player see it. The first player then describes the picture to the second player – "This is a picture of a tree and a house, and the house is on the left of . . . " and the second player tries to draw as close a replica as possible. The first player is guiding the second player's hand with their voice alone. No hand or body signals allowed. It's fun to compare pictures when finished. After one picture is completed, reverse roles.

ICE CUBE TOSS – Fill a cooler full of ice cubes. Place a bucket five or six feet away. Toss ice cubes from the cooler to the bucket or if a group of children, toss ice cubes back and forth in teams until ice cube melts.

This 'N That

When children must share a closet, prevent arguments over space by painting each half a different color. Paint clothes hangers to match each child's side.

Instead of discarding yarn, lint from your dryer, cotton string, mops, etc., leave it outside for the birds during early spring. They will pick out the strands for nest building.

Drink a glass of carrot juice every day before going to the beach. It has been known to increase your tan in a shorter period of time.

At hair-washing time, keep shampoo out of children's eyes by giving them underwater goggles to wear.

Put baby's high chair in the shower for a few minutes and it will take care of cleaning up the mess with very little scrubbing.

When a youngster refuses to wear the clothing you pick out, lay three outfits out on the bed side-by-side. Then let the child select what to wear. Having a choice makes all the difference.

After a day at the beach, remove the last traces of sand from the body or feet by sprinkling on talcum powder and rubbing lightly with a towel. The sand will vanish as if by magic.

When children begin to complain that they are too old for babysitters, working mothers might try this solution during the summer months. Hire an "entertainer director" – a teenager with enough skill and interest to take the children to the library, supervise crafts, cooking, swimming pool, etc.

Soften ice cream by microwaving at 30% power. One pint will take 15 to 30 seconds, one quart, 30 to 45 seconds.

NOTES

ABOUT THE AUTHOR

Diane Sand was raised on a family farm near Elberon, Iowa. She grew up with a mother who was – and still is – always working on some kind of "project". Her father patiently tolerated living in a household overflowing in the activities of a wife and three daughters.

Diane has a degree in Business Education from the University of Northern Iowa. She has spent most of her adult life working out of her home while raising four children. The Sand family has been transferred around the country settling in Lilburn, Georgia, a suburb of Atlanta. Each of the four children was born in a different state.

The celebration of special events continues in the Sand household. Diane and Larry have combined travel and celebration by celebrating each of their 27 anniversaries in a different state.

The family has been blessed with the opportunity to celebrate two very special occasions – the Golden Anniversary of Larry's parents, Leo and Norene Sand last year and the anticipation of the upcoming Golden Anniversary of Diane's parents, Delmer and Kathryn Brunssen.

FOR ORDERING ADDITIONAL BOOKS

DLS SERVICES
4157 Signal Ridge Drive
Lilburn, GA 30047

770-978-4712

"How To Be A Super Room Mother, Team Mom, Scout Leader, Sunday School Teacher, Etc. Etc. Etc."
DLS Services
4157 Signal Ridge Drive
Lilburn GA 30047
770-978-4712

Please send _____ copies of your book at $14.95 per copy. I have included $2.00 per copy for postage and handling. Enclosed is my check or money order for $_____.

Name: _____

Address: _____

City, State, Zip: _____

"How To Be A Super Room Mother, Team Mom, Scout Leader, Sunday School Teacher, Etc. Etc. Etc."
DLS Services
4157 Signal Ridge Drive
Lilburn GA 30047
770-978-4712

Please send _____ copies of your book at $14.95 per copy. I have included $2.00 per copy for postage and handling. Enclosed is my check or money order for $_____.

Name: _____

Address: _____

City, State, Zip: _____